NORTH DAKOTA
STATE UNIVERSITY
AUG 0 8 1984
SERIALS DEPT.
LIBRARY

WITHDRAWN

THEATRE LIBRARY ASSOCIATION

The Theatre Library Association is a non-profit organization established in 1937 to advance the interests of all those involved in collecting and preserving theatrical materials and in utilizing those materials for purposes of scholarship. The membership is international and includes public and private institutions as well as librarians, curators, private collectors, historians, professors, theatre designers, actors, writers, and all other interested persons.

The Theatre Library Association meets annually to conduct its business in the fall of each year. It presents a day of conferences and programs during the annual meeting of the American Library Association, usually in late spring or early summer.

Its publications are Broadside, *a quarterly newsletter, and* Performing Arts Resources, *an annual journal.*

It is governed by a constitution which provides for a board of directors elected by the membership and officers elected by the board.

1984 OFFICERS AND BOARD MEMBERS

Dorothy L. Swerdlove, President
Curator, The Billy Rose Theatre
 Collection
The New York Public Library,
New York

Mary Ann Jensen, Vice-President
Curator, Theatre Collection
Princeton University

Richard M. Buck,
Secretary-Treasurer
Performing Arts Research Center,
The New York Public Library

Brigitte Kueppers,
Recording Secretary
Archivist, Shubert Archive
Lyceum Theatre, New York

William Appleton
New York City

Elizabeth Burdick
Librarian,
International Theatre Institute
New York

Geraldine Duclow
Librarian in Charge,
Theatre Collection
Free Library of Philadelphia

Gerald Kahan
Department of Drama and Theatre
University of Georgia

Martha Mahard
Assistant Curator,
Theatre Collection
Harvard University

Julian Mates
Dean, School of the Arts
C.W. Post Center,
Long Island University

Lois Ericson McDonald
Associate Curator,
The O'Neill Theatre Center

Robert L. Parkinson
Circus World Museum Library
Baraboo, Wisconsin

Louis A. Rachow
Librarian-Curator,
Hampden-Booth Collection,
The Players Club

Elizabeth Ross
The Billy Rose Theatre Collection,
The New York Public Library

Anne G. Schlosser
Head Librarian,
American Film Institute
Louis B. Mayer Library
Beverly Hills, California

Alan Woods
Director,
Theatre Research Institute
The Ohio State University

EX OFFICIO
Ginnine Cocuzza
Co-Editor,
Performing Arts Resources

Barbara Naomi Cohen-Stratyner
Co-Editor,
Performing Arts Resources

Alan J. Pally
Editor, *Broadside*

Don B. Wilmeth
Brown University
Awards Committee

HONORARY
Rosamond Gilder
Paul Myers

THE THEATRE LIBRARY ASSOCIATION BOOK AWARDS

Two awards are presented annually for books of unusual merit and distinction in the fields served by the Association.

The George Freedley Award, *established in 1968, honors work in the field of theatre published in the United States. Only books with subjects related to live performance will be considered. They may be biography, history or criticism.*

The Theatre Library Association Award, *established in 1973, honors a book published in the United States in the field of recorded performance, which includes motion pictures, radio and television.*

Works ineligible for both awards are textbooks; anthologies; collections of essays previously published in other sources; reprints; works on dance, ballet and opera; plays and similar dramatic works. Translations of significant works, other than play texts, will be considered. Entries will be judged on the basis of scholarship, readability and general contribution of knowledge to the fields served by the Association. No galley sheets or proofs will be accepted. Books nominated for awards must be published in the calendar year prior to the presentation of the awards and must be received no later than March 1 of the year following publication.

Nominations are to be submitted in writing to the Chair, Book Awards Committee, in care of the Theatre Library Association, 111 Amsterdam Avenue, New York, N.Y. 10023.

PERFORMING ARTS RESOURCES, *the annual publication of the Theatre Library Association, is designed to gather and disseminate scholarly articles dealing with the location of resource materials relating to theatre, film, television and radio; descriptions, listings, or evaluations of the contents of such collections, whether public or private; and monographs of previously unpublished original source material.*

All manuscripts to be submitted must be typed cleanly, on one side only, double-spaced and adhering to the style and method described in the MLA Style Sheet, Second Edition. *Photographs and other illustrations will be used at the discretion of the editors.*

Please submit manuscripts with covering letter and return postage to:

Performing Arts Resources
c/o B. N. Cohen-Stratyner
300 Riverside Drive
New York, New York 10025

PERFORMING ARTS RESOURCES

Edited by Ginnine Cocuzza
and
Barbara Naomi Cohen-Stratyner

VOLUME NINE

Published by the Theatre Library Association

Copyright © 1984 by the Theatre Library Association
Headquarters: 111 Amsterdam Avenue, New York, NY 10023
Membership dues: $20 personal, $25 institutional

Introduction and translation
copyright © 1983 by Alfred Siemon Golding

The Library of Congress catalogued this serial as follows:
Performing Arts Resources
    Vols. for 1974—issued by the Theatre Library Association
    ISSN 0360-3814
1. Performing arts—Library resources—United States-Periodicals.
I. Theatre Library Association
Z6935.P46   016.7902'08   75-646287
ISBN 0-932610-06-4

*Produced by BookCrafters, Inc., Chelsea, Michigan
Manufactured in the United States of America*

TABLE OF CONTENTS

From the Editors   ix

Introduction   xiii

An Essay on Stage Performance:
   A Translation of Franz Lang's
   Dissertatio de Actione Scenica (1727)   1

Symbolic Images especially Useful in
   Theatrical Performance and Costuming   71

Illustrations reproduced by permission of the British Library

FROM THE EDITORS

We are pleased to add Alfred Siemon Golding's translation of Franz Lang's *Dissertatio de Actione Scenica* to the *Performing Arts Resources* series published by the Theatre Library Association. Lang's *Essay on Stage Performance* and its appended listing of Symbolic Images will prove invaluable to scholars, performers and designers interested in Baroque theater.

Lang's *Essay*, written originally as a text for his students at the Jesuit Gymnasium of Munich, focuses on natural movement and grace in acting. His instructions have an internal logic and kinesthetic sense that will make the *Essay* useful for students of movement of the 18th century, as well as those scholars who specialize in texts of the period. Lang also includes his theories on vocal presentation and takes sides in the controversy among those who tried to maintain the classical unities and those who wished to modernize the drama.

We have followed Lang's *Essay* with an appendix of Symbolic Images especially Useful in Theatrical Performance and Costuming. His descriptions of allegorical figures from "Absentinentia a malo" to "Zyphyr" are fascinating studies of iconographics in transition between Greek and Roman mythology and Baroque visualizations.

To facilitate the modern reader's comprehension of the documents, we have simplified Lang's complicated system of footnotes and divided them into a list of conventional reference citations and a glossary of the names to whom he refered. Notes in the Symbolic Images section have been integrated into the text.

Alfred S. Golding has been a professor in the Department of Theatre at Ohio State University since 1973. An historian and specialist in theatre documentation and performing arts libraries and museums, he served for some years as Director of the Department's Theatre Research Institute. Presently Dr. Golding teaches advanced courses in theatre history, his area of emphasis being the Baroque theatre and its acting methods.

Dr. Golding received his B.A. *cum laude* from the City College of New York, an M.F.A. from Yale University and a Ph.D. from Columbia University. He has taught at his *alma mater*, Western Connecticut State College and the University of South Florida, directing more than one hundred plays at these institutions. He is the author of numerous scholarly articles and translations, and of two books, *Class-*

icistic Acting and, with Professor André Veinstein, *Performing Arts Libraries and Museums of the World* (Third Edition). He is presently Vice President of the International Association of Performing Arts Libraries and Museums. Dr. Golding has been the holder of a grant from the National Endowment for the Humanities, a Fellow of the American Council for Learned Societies, and a member of the board of Directors of the Theatre Library Association.

The Editors and the Theatre Library Association wish to thank the staff and directors of The British Library for their invaluable assistance. The translation of the original manuscript and reproduction of illustrations herein are made by permission of The British Library. We also wish to thank Edith Abel for her keen eye and proof reading expertise.

Performing Arts Resources will continue to make available reference material to augment library collections and give researchers access to rare material as well as articles and essays that will enable librarians, archivists and scholars to locate, identify and classify information on theatre, film, broadcasting and popular entertainment. Our next volume will focus on performing arts company archives. Projected columes include sheet music holdings, dance resources and film technology. We welcome our readers' comments and suggestions.

Ginnine Cocuzza
Barbara Naomi Cohen-Stratyner

An Essay on Stage Performance:
A Translation of Franz Lang's
Dissertatio de Actione Scenica (1727)

by Alfred Siemon Golding

LANG'S "ESSAY ON STAGE PERFORMANCE": AN INTRODUCTION

During the eighteenth century one of the first books to appear on acting as a distinctive art was published under Jesuit imprimatur. Its author was a well-known professor of rhetoric and director of theatre performance in Bavaria. For more than fifty years, Father Franz Lang, S.J. (1654–1725) taught acting and directed and wrote plays in the schools of the Jesuit Order. His "Essay on Stage Performance" (*Dissertatio de actione scenica*),[1] published in 1727, has long been recognized in Europe as a document of importance to the study of acting of the Baroque and incipient Rococo periods.[2] In order to make the work accessible to theatre students in America who may be unfamiliar with Baroque Latin, the work has been translated into English.[3]

In the last decades of the seventeenth century when Father Lang supervised theatre activities in the Jesuit Gymnasium of Munich, the goals of the Counter-Reformation which had originally brought the Society of Jesus and its theatre into being had largely been displaced by those of education. The time was one of upward mobility for the Bavarian middle class, and its members sent their sons to the Jesuit gymnasia to receive gentlemanly instruction which would enable them to mix in polite society. In consequence the study of rhetoric loomed large in the curriculum. While learning to speak and write well, pupils also received training in how to stand, move, walk and talk as did persons of quality. Even before the Renaissance, theatrical exercises, such as the presentation of dramatic monologues, short scenes and long plays in Latin, had constituted tests of declamatory ability, poise and decorum for students of the *trivium* in the schools of Europe. In effect, acting (which demonstrated heroic and ignoble conduct) was taught under a rhetorical rubric. The customary practice had its counterpart in poetry and playwriting (*poësis*) which were then taught under the written aspect of rhetoric. During the Renaissance as well, the five canons of rhetoric were recombined and studied as individual subjects, in great measure because of a new interest in logicality and in the pursuit of specialized knowledge. Less touched by the puritanical tendency of Ramism which shifted a traditional rhetoric towards logic and written discourse, the Jesuits continued to assert the primacy of emotionality in persuasion and so to emphasize in their rhetoric the spoken word, symbolism and theatricality. In their pedagogic zeal they too began to specialize, producing books on the content and method of delivery (*pronuntiatio*), the fourth rhetorical canon, as it was practiced by the cultivated members of society. Lang's "Essay" may thus be seen as an extension of this specialized interest in delivery manifested by his predecessors (albeit for the theatre), and a reflection of the performance standards and methods conventional to the theatre of his time.[4]

In his descriptions of platform behavior for the stage player, Lang drew upon classical sources originally conceived for the orator, as confirmed by Jesuit authorities and his own experience.[5] Like other teachers of rhetoric he saw it under a dual aspect of speaking and writing, and so divided his "Essay" into corresponding sections dealing with acting and playwriting. Although as a practical man of the theatre he felt the need to incorporate materials on the mounting of a production, he sensed the danger of departing too far from an accepted format. Thus he contented himself with creating a rhetorical sourcebook for the inexperienced Jesuit *choragus* (supervisor of theatre activities).

Lang's slim volume was nevertheless in its own way a radical innovation in its assumption that acting was, despite its rhetorical base, an art *sui generis* with its special rule of deportment and characterization. For scholarly analysis has revealed that the attitudes, for example, which Lang depicted in his illustrations and described in his text extended beyond the practice of rhetoric to other disciplines as well. They serve to inform us about the grand manner of the nobility at court, the no less egregious conduct of the tragedians and comedians of the professional troupes, and indeed the heroic posturing exhibited by the figures of Baroque sculpture and painting.[6] There is also evidence to indicate that deportment, at least in the style presented by Lang in the "Essay" and his productions, was too theatrical to suit the tastes of some of his superiors. He was, apparently, challenging an earlier and more constrained rational manner of playing that was no longer fashionable with the theatre-going public but was still favored by the Society's conservative leadership.[7]

Lang wrote the "Essay" in the final years of his life when he was suffering from a debilitating illness. Perhaps for this reason his writing seems somewhat disorganized and the author hesitated even at the last to make a definitive printed statement in defiance of an established view. Yet Lang obviously also chose his words with care, and these may be used to fathom his intention. So in the title of his work the term *dissertatio* could have the same meaning as its English cognate does today—an extensive and detailed discussion of a topic. But the word also could designate a tentative and incomplete account of a little explored area of study—hence in modern parlance an "essay." A similar review of the third word of the title, *actio*, and the fourth, its modifier *scenica*, leads to the conclusion that Lang deliberately employed a term of rhetoric so as not to depart too far from a traditional base. *Actio*, after all, was but another word for *pronuntiatio* or delivery; hence in utilizing the term he was, for appearances at least, simply extending the fourth canon of rhetoric to the stage. It must be remembered as well that in Lang's time *actio* did not have the same meaning that "acting" has for the present day—a word neither encumbered nor enhanced by rhetorical linkage. In Baroque Latin *orator* and *actor* were nearly synonymous and their vernacular equivalents were regularly used to honor a "common player" [*histrio*] of distinction by bestowing upon him a rhetorical title. Thus the translator has rendered the first words of Lang's title as an "Essay on Stage Performance" to indicate the delicacy of Lang's word selection that hints at rather than declares acting to be an art apart from rhetoric, although the contents of the "Essay" reveal this to be his theme.

Lang's avoidance of any treatment of stage symbolism also invites comment. Such activity was so fundamental to Baroque performance that it apparently required no justification or elaboration. For the modern reader, the methods practiced in symbolic delivery may require a word of explanation. The art of the Baroque orator/actor lay in the skills with which he revealed the outer signs of inner feeling. After initial training in imitating a repertory of conventional emotional expressions, he was expected to "invent" (according to the first canon of rhetoric) his own modification appropriate to the style and substance of his discourse. The process was not mechanical because he recalled these earlier learned expressions in the form of mental images in order to produce them overtly. To an audience such symbolic behavior seemed natural because they were familiar with these conventions of expressing emotion and so could readily recognize them. Much practice in attitudinizing, gesticulation and the play of the features and the voice made the performance graceful and true-to-life.

Prior to his public appearance the orator/actor arranged the sequence of these expressions to conform to the flow of his thoughts, memorizing the physical action appropriate to the words he was to declaim. In performance the orator (although for brief moments) and the actor (for the duration of his appearance on stage) assumed the identity of another person (or thing) by employing the rhetorical device of *personatio* or impersonation to enliven his discourse by making himself seem to be what he was not. In this multi-dimensional style of speaking and acting the performer could represent himself on several levels at once—as an imitation of a lifelike character, as a symbol of what that character stood for, and as the actual speaker/player beneath the characterization. In this symbolic construct, the actor's figurative behavior augmented the playwright's poetry in the same way that the orator's figures of action enlarged upon the figures of speech of his discourse.

It is precisely in this regard that Lang's catalogue of symbolic images proves instructive. For his juxtaposition of a battery of descriptions of emblematic figures with acting and writing suggests that the congeries of scenic illusion and allusion of the Baroque drama resonated their themes much as did the orator/actor: as a laminate of congruent symbols whose hidden meaning was gradually disclosed only through performance. Lang's notes on the manner of costuming and positioning allegorical figures can enrich present understanding of the process of hermetic figurativeness in the Baroque theatre. For these images he drew upon two traditional sources. The first was Cesare Ripa's *Inconologia*, originally issued in 1593 and much reprinted in many languages and illustrated with pictures. The second was Jakob Masen's *Speculum imaginum veritatis occulatae* ("Figures Reflecting Hidden Truth"), written for the Jesuit stage in 1650 and republished no less than eight times before the end of the century.

Lang produced his plays upon a stage somewhat smaller and less well furnished than that of the Munich Court Theatre, yet much like it in its basic arrangements. The Gymnasium's stage was a temporary structure erected in its assembly hall [*aula*], equipped for quick scenic transformations and flying effects. The perspective settings were disposed in the usual wing-border format with backcloths at the rear and shutters half-way upstage. Scenes were painted in the fashion of generalized exterior and interior views also characterstic of the Baroque theatre of court. Lang's plays reveal that he characteristically alternated a full-stage playing area with another downstage of the intermediary shutter and designed his dramatic locales to accord with the content of the scene dock.[8]

Lang's pragmatic approach to his craft stemmed from a lifetime of activity in the Jesuit theatre. As a student at the Munich Gymnasium (from 1661–1671) he took part in several plays. Upon graduation he entered the Order and, after five years of additional course work, began to teach rhetoric and so to write and direct plays for use by his students in the classroom. In 1679 Lang was favored by being allowed to prepare the major plays which were annually presented at the end of the school year before an invited audience. In 1694 he was named to the post of Prefect of Studies and President of the Greater Marian Congregation. For the sodality he created several programs of dramatized meditations which were staged at seasonal holidays.[9] During the last ten years of his life he catalogued the collection of theatre programs in the archives of the College's library. In these final years he also penned the "Essay on Stage Performance," but permission to publish came too late for him to see his work in print. Father Lang died in 1725; his "Essay" appeared two years later.

In his theory and practice Lang espoused a sensibility characteristic not so much of the school production as that of the professional theatre of his own day. As a teacher he demonstrated that the art of acting, like that of rhetoric, was subject to methodical explanation. Although his playwriting was largely derivative, his acting method, as is evident in the "Essay on Stage Performance," displays the craftsmanship which made his productions appealing to his students and the pubic who saw his presentations. By delineating some fundamental techniques which the actor was expected to know when performing on the Jesuit stage, Lang left as a legacy a significant textbook for students of Baroque theatre history.

Notes: Introduction

[1] In full, *Dissertatio de actione scenica, cum figuris eandem explicantibus, et observationibus quibusdam de arte comica. Auctore P. Francisco Lang Societatis Jesu. Accesserunt imagines symbolicae pro exhibitione et vestitu theatrali.* It has been translated as: "Essay on Stage Performance with Illustrations of the Same, and containing some Observations on the Art of Playwriting by Father Franciscus Lang, S.J. To which have been added Symbolic Figures for use in Theatrical Performance and Costume."
[2] The first modern reference to the "Essay" was made by Karl von Reinhardstöttner in his article, "Zur Geschichte des Jesuitendramas in München," *Jahrbuch für Munchener Geschichte*, III (1889). Nicholas Scheid was the first to recognize the "Essay" as an early treatment of the art of acting in his "P. Franciscus Langs Büchlein über die Schauspielkunst, Ein Beitrag zur Jesuitendramatik," *Euphorion: Zeitschrift für Theatergeschicte*, VIII (1901). More recently Lang's "Essay" has constituted a major source for the reconstruction of Baroque acting style in Willi Flemming's "Die Erfassung des Epochalstils barocker Schauspielkunst in Deutschland," *Maske and Kothurn* I (1955), and in Winfried Klara's *Schauspielkostüm und Schauspieldarstellung, Schriften der Gesellschaft für Theatergeschicte* XLIII (1931).
[3] The major published references in English which discuss Lang's volume are Ronald G. Engle's "Lang's Discourse on Stage Movement," *Educational Theatre Journal*, XXII,2 (1970), and Alfred S. Golding's "A Baroque Theory of Acting and Playwriting as Symbolic Representation: Lang's 'Essay on Stage Performance' (1727)" in *Theatre Studies*, XXI (1974/5).
[4] For a history of the Jesuit theatre, particularly in German-speaking countries, see Willi Flemming, *Geschichte des Jesuitentheaters in den Landen deutscher Zunge, Schriften der Gesellschaft für Theatergeschichte* XXXII (1923). A brief survey of the Jesuit theatre may be found in Henry Schnitzler's "The School Theatre of the Jesuits," *Theatre Annual* (1944), and in his "The Jesuit Contribution to the Theatre," *Educational Theatre Journal*, IV,4 (1952).

The most comprehensive of the texts on delivery written under Jesuit auspices was Louis Crésol's *Vacationes autumnales, sive de Perfecta oratoris actione et pronuntiatione* (1620) which became the basis for a number of important works of oratory and acting, although Lang seems not to have made use of its contents. Nor did he apparently use Jodocus Willich's *Pronuntiatione rhetorica doctus et elegans* (1540). He did utilize as a source Jean Voël's *Artificium generale texendae sive componendae orationis* (1589), Nicholas Caussin's *De Eloquentia sacra et humana* (1617), Johannes Lucas' *Actio orationis* (1675) and Joseph de Jouvency's *Ratio discendi et docendi* (1685)—specifically the *Ratio pronunciando* (II,9 of the work), much of which he paraphrased.

During the late seventeenth and early eighteenth centuries the Munich Court frequently invited reputable English, French, Dutch and Italian companies to perform before it. Of the non-German companies the most famous was that led by Francesco Calderone (Silvio), and, of the German, that led by Johannes Velten. See Karl Trautmann, "Deutsche Schauspieler am Bayerischen Hofe," *Jahrbuch für Müchener Geschichte*, III(1889).

[5]These were Marcus Fabianus Quintilian's *Institutes of Oratory* and Marcus Tullius Cicero's *Orator*, in particular, works from which Jesuit works on delivery drew many of their precepts and examples. Lang also cited these ancient authorities to validate his own practice.

[6]There is good evidence that seventeenth and early eighteenth century actors shared a conventional aesthetic behavior with painters and sculptors as well as orators. The *contraposto* posture mandated by Lang, for example, for stage personages of distinction is found in Burnacini's sculpture and designs for presentations at the Viennese court, the portraits of French nobles done by the court painters according to the principles of the Royal Academy and the works of oratorial delivery. See in this regard Alexander Rudin, *Franciscus Lang und die Schaubühne, Die Schaubühne* LXXII (1973).

[7]Lang's plays were denied publication and both his "Dramatic Meditations" and his "Essay" were delayed in receiving an official imprimatur, despite Lang's manifest popularity. After his death his "Essay" was deliberately ignored by the leaders of the Society. In 1736 an ordinance appeared under the signature of the head of the Jesuit school system for southern Germany and Switzerland, directing its playmakers to look to the more restrained advice of Jouvency on delivery in a work then over fifty years old, although copies of Lang's work were readily available in the Jesuit libraries.

[8]Werner Kindig, *Franz Lang: Ein Jesuitendramatiker der Spätbarock* (unpublished doctoral dissertation, University of Graz, Austria, 1965), 95–105.

[9]The *Bibliothèque de la Compagnie de Jesu* of Backer/Sommervogel on pages 1478–1480 lists Lang's seven plays, three dramatic meditations and other works. The meditations were presented in the newly reconstructed oratio of St. Michael's Church, Munich. Following earlier Jesuit practice Lang divided the upstage areas into three compartments which could be concealed or revealed by drawn curtains. These areas could be used for pantomimic interludes, or miraculous appearances by means of flying apparatus. Downstage, emblems mounted on small wagons could be pushed from the wings at propitious moments into the audience's view.

Dissertatio de Actione Scenica, Cum Figuris eandem Explicantibus, Et Observationibus Quibusdam De Arte Comica.	An Essay on Stage Performance, With Illustrations of the Same And Containing Some Observations on the Art of Playwriting.
Auctore P. Francisco Lang, Societatis Jesu.	By Father Franz Lang S.J.
Accesserunt imagines symbolicae Pro exhibitione et vestitu theatrali.	To Which Have Been Added Symbolic Figures For Use in Theatrical Performance and Costuming.
Superiorum Permissu, Sumptibus Joan Andreae de la Haye, Bibliopolae Academici Ingolstadii.	With the Permission of his Superiors And at the Expense of John Andrea de la Haye, Bibliopole of the Ingolstadt Academy.
Monachii, Typis Mariae Magdalene Riedlin, Viduae, 1727.	Printed at Munich by Maria Magdalene Riedlin, Widow, 1727.

FOREWORD

Many people have often asked me to record what I consider to be the principles and practices of stage performance for the purpose of educating young men in cultural pursuits. They have especially urged me to do so, they said, because this noble and essential art has never been before rendered into printed form. For Aristotle and that prince of orators, Cicero, have left the task for us to complete, since they only treat delivery and vocal inflection and pay scant attention to the systematic management of the body, considered in its total aspect and in its parts, for public speaking. Certainly they have not written extensively enough to satisfy discriminating students of that art. More recently, some writers have also promulgated some rules for gesture and platform behavior,[1] but these rules were not specifically intended for theatrical use.

In undertaking the present task I am hardly suggesting that I am a qualified final authority or that my essay is the definitive work on acting. On the contrary, I recognize the task as too much for any one man. I know as well my own serious shortcomings and, of course, the major problems of publication which require capability and perseverance beyond my own resources.

Then too, in this corrupt age what man dares to suggest that he can impart new wisdom? If something new is said especially about an old subject, the statement is forthwith declared an error, an obvious falsehood, or a piece of persiflage. The ancient classic songs dampen enthusiasm for new tunes. The consequences for one who labors to do what has not been done before, therefore, are cavil, contempt and general derision.

I am also well aware that those for whom my essay is intended—those amateurs who produce plays and those who participate in them—are few in number. Exempt the teachers of rhetoric and poetics in the Gymnasia, and the number of those who might consult the work out of curiosity or sincere desire for knowledge is so minute as to hardly justify the expenditure for publication.

What publisher would underwrite so expensive a work on a subject of only scholarly interest and which is unmarketable? And if there is no demand, a small book rests idly, gathering dust on the shelves of the bookstore, a clear loss to the bookseller.

There is, in addition, the difficult problem of having to explain in explicit language a subject like stage performance which is far removed from ordinary behavior. The reader must obtain from the sense of the writing a knowledge of how to turn the whole body so that its movements, steps and strides, its positions and postures will follow as a matter of course and so that either he or those whom he is teaching may form an accurate impression.

May not a skillfully executed drawing accomplish the purpose of revealing the rules of acting and gesturing artistically? I grant that an illustration can communicate much about the subject. But there is also a sizeable gap between the lifelessness of a figure on paper and the vitality of the human body as a means of demonstration. In this regard I recognize as well that my text is equally deficient.

If my essay were to be circulated in manuscript form and not printed, it would reach only a few readers. How many then would take the trouble to prepare a handwritten copy for themselves or for others? But a clearly printed version can be distributed and read more easily than a carelessly or illegibly handwritten manuscript particularly for the benefit of those who genuinely wish to study the art seriously, rather than to only casually learn about it. It is silly to take unwilling hounds a-hunting.[2]

Of course, authors who burn the midnight oil to prepare a manuscript for the printer face other difficulties also. They must be solitary, rejecting all aid and subjecting themselves to the pain of writing, preferring to hide themselves in silence and to undergo the irksomeness, the tedium and the travail of birth in order to bring their creation to light, although its publication may make them suspect and even lead to their condemnation.

Up to this moment these considerations have deterred me from this labor. But I have now reflected upon the matter more carefully and have resolved to dedicate my spare time to record the precepts of acting for the benefit of those who are students of the art of the stage, and especially for the greater glory of GOD, for whose sake our theatre has been constructed and equipped. These rules derive partly from the examples of other experts in the field, and partly from my own study in many years of practical experience.

The purpose of this labor of mine, therefore, is to gratify the wishes of my petitioners and of all others, whomever they may be. I do so at least to illuminate the subject for the first time, so that they may perfect themselves in stage performance and, by the pleasure inspired by theatrical production, move an audience to faith and duty. If perchance this modest effort should obtain favor, others more expert in the art may be encouraged to follow and to build a complete structure upon my rude foundation. For every beginning is imperfect. With the help of God I have labored to frame these lines for my own use. If anyone who reads them deems them of value, let him acknowledge that such profit as he derives is from God's goodness, and, by way of gratitude, let him remember me in his prayers.

CHAPTER I

OF STAGE ACTION, ITS DEFINITION AND VALUE

It is really unnecessary to discuss the value of bodily action in delivery, since expert authority commends it highly, in addition to common sense and experience. For bodily activity has been very highly endorsed for ancient orators on the rostrum out of doors and for more modern speakers who occupy an indoor pulpit. Yet in both instances only half of their bodies was visible. Then should it not be judged suitable for actors on the stage, where the entire body and its individual parts are fully revealed in order to render the emotions in an appropriate fashion for an audience? Let me state quite boldly that the total action of the body is such a marvelous force for exciting the emotions that the play director [*choragus*] who himself is skilled in bodily action, or who knows how to instruct others in the art, can bend an audience to his will. But not to digress, I shall limit myself to describing the characteristics of stage action. It is the art of modifying the entire body in a fashion calculated to create feeling in an audience. Acting, therefore, involves a control of the postures and movements of the body and of the modulations of the voice. It makes use of the laws of art and nature in order to give pleasure through arousing the affections.

CHAPTER II

CONCERNING THE NECESSITY FOR ART IN ACTING OR WHETHER NATURE ALONE SUFFICES

To achieve perfection in performance an actor must have natural ability and must also achieve a mastery of his craft. I may be criticized in this regard by some who say that natural genius is sufficient—in their words acting must be natural. Therefore, they continue, no rules of art ought to be given the student because they are useless, superfluous and a hindrance to the truly creative artist.

However, if the matter be thought through most carefully, I believe these critics will come round to my view. Let us begin by recalling the origins and purposes of the arts in general. In their initial state such efforts were feeble, crude and imperfect. In due course the arts came under the purview of men of discernment. From the most craftsmanlike of these activities the experts have formulated laws and precepts which since have enabled novices in the arts to achieve mastery wth greater surety and less chance for error. We see this more particularly in the manual and in the liberal arts. In both we can discern a fundamental talent in man glowing dully at first, but with use shining more brightly, and if allowed extensive cultivation, achieving brilliant perfection. Thus, at first men handled hammers, saws and chisels unskillfully. Then after they had constructed many objects, they developed the art of carpentry and ultimately architecture. And similarly with regard to painting, sculpture and other handicrafts.

The same is true if we should speak of the sciences which were developed from mental activity. The first glimmerings of knowledge came from natural inspiration. But only after these vague and unformed pieces of information had been studied by observant men was knowledge organized and reduced into a perfect system. We sense that basically every man has some small natural insight into theology, law, dialectic and rhetoric, and if needs be can argue these subjects in a rough and ready way. For example, a beggar may plead eloquently out of his misery in order to obtain a donation, and a peasant may employ natural common sense in a crude way in order to defend himself although ignorant of jurisprudence which should properly be utilized in a case of law. As a result each man deduces one truth from the other and so reaches a conclusion favorable to himself. That men have some knowledge must be acknowledged as a natural gift. But their lack of perfect knowledge has to be attributed to an inadequacy of systematic training in the subject.

Now to apply this principle to acting. Experience teaches us that movements of the hands and other limbs come about naturally. By such action man animates his conversation and produces a more vital communication than can be effected by words alone. But on this level these motions are rude and uncultivated. Man must now become more effective through artistry: to reach his objective he must refine the manner of his expression. And as the sciences and the manual arts are improved through systematic cultivation, so it is also with acting. For acting is nothing else but the representation of customary behavior of characters conceived by a play-maker [*choragus*] for exhibition in a theatre. To continue, acting wholly and completely by natural instinct cannot produce an excellent performance. To do so requires careful preparation. The actions of the characters must be given considerable study which involves first conceiving them well in the mind before assuming them exactly in bodily and vocal form. This is the proper exercise of art.

In its *modus operandi* acting resembles the way in which a story is imagined and shaped for theatrical performance by a playwright. For just as he twists and turns related events of a plot in a pleasantly involved and varied fashion by a happy faculty of invention and felicitous arrangement, so he also nicely molds the expressions needed, in general, for realizing the personalities of his characters. Playacting thus renders in theatrical terms the same manner of behavior originally conceived for the play in its written form. Everyone recognizes what a difficult business it is to create a work of art. In the first instance dramatic characters do not possess the same qualities as do those of history. For example, the character of Medea by Seneca was not the historic character who was the daughter of Aeëta, King of Colchis, but a fictional entity conceived for the stage. Seneca made the words and actions of his imagined Medea seem appropriate, not that the historic Medea literally spoke the words or performed the actions supplied by the playwright while she was killing her sons, but because, mad with rage and vengeance, a fictional Medea, in all probability, would talk and act in such a fashion. In the second instance, to write a play in which effects follow causes as they do in nature is generally regarded as an extraordinary artistic achievement. It is the product of much learning and practice in youth and of unremitting toil in maturity. In other words, what a playwright creates as fiction must still be in conformity to nature: he must frame words of his characters to fit their feelings as these would naturally be expressed. In just such a way the actor, following the work of the playwright, shows the emotions of his character on stage by imitating their overt appearance as these appear and change over his entire body. To act in such a fashion is the hallmark of artistry.

From the foregoing I believe it is abundantly clear that acting requires the highest technical competency, for perfect representation cannot exist without artistic discipline. As was marked by Julius Caesar Scalinger in his *Poetices* (Book I, Chapter 13), *a stage character is an imitation of a real human being created in the imagination of the playwright for performance in a theatre.*[3] As has been demonstrated many times in this regard, if some precept of art is forthcoming which is not generally known, it should not be dismissed summarily as fantastic, an error, or an affectation; even though it is less imitative of nature, it still has value if it contributes a sense of style and harmony of effect. The reader may trust me when I say this, for by dint of long experience I have discovered the proof of what I say by actual practice. Having established my position, I can now proceed to a discussion of basic acting principles.

CHAPTER III

CONCERNING THE RULES FOR LEARNING HOW TO ACT AND WHAT BODILY PART SHOULD BE SUBJECT TO DISCIPLINE

Lest the reader now think that what I have to say about acting is a product of my own imagination, I claim support from that very nature which was the first teacher of mankind, and from sculpture, painting, and the other fine arts which are universally honored and given individual attention in Rome the ruler of the world. I can also cite those who have been patrons and teachers of the discipline of acting. From their artistic records, particularly their engravings which are generally admired and enjoyed, I derive proof and authority for my statements. If I follow their rules and axioms in training the body for expression, I cannot be accused of being audacious or vain.

According to their teachings, therefore, we may now direct our attention to the correct fashion of moving the body and precisely arranging its separate parts, from which proceed all artistic action. We shall initially review the stance of the legs and the feet, the disposition of the knees, the posture of the legs while at rest and in motion, the way in which the hips, shoulders and trunk of the body are held, the arms, elbows and hands and then the movements of the neck, head, face and eyes. Each part will be described in its static and dynamic aspects after which speech and its relation to physical action will be treated. Having introduced the order by which the body parts are presented to the student for his government and separate mastery, I may properly begin to discuss my subject.

CHAPTER IV

CONCERNING THE STANCE OF THE BODY AND OF THE LOWER LIMBS

The first topic, the stance and the lower limbs, must commence with the statement that on the stage the feet should never be set out in parallel alignment, but always angled somewhat, so that the toes are pointed in different directions. I call this position of the feet in performance the acting angle [*crux scenica*], for purposes of clarification. To render this more visible than can be done with words I have appended a drawing of the position (Figure I). This first picture, however, provides an example of poor stage posture, that is, a position which an actor should not assume. Consider in the illustration the way in which the feet have been placed almost in a straight line when they should have been turned out. Consequently, the body position seems weak and the actor stands stupidly like a lifeless statue. In addition, the arms, elbows and hands are inelegantly arranged. But I shall dwell upon this point later. Suffice it to say that the movements of the hands and arms should not be made near the midline of the body, or below the belt, nor should the arms be extended in exactly the same fashion, nor the elbows and upper arms be held in close to the trunk, nor should the fingers and open palms be extended stiffly. But now let us turn our attention to the feet, not only while standing, but in walking and in traversing on the stage.

First a warning: on stage the feet should never be set out perfectly aligned and parallel with each other. Rather the first should be turned out obliquely so that it is diagonal to the second—that is, one foot angled to the right and the other to the left. At the same time, one foot should be placed somewhat forward of the other. If this is done correctly the body will never be in a single unbroken plane, and will always be turned more or less in the direction of the audience. Of necessity, when each foot is properly set in this fashion, the posture of the rest of the body will naturally follow in an appropriate way. For the foot must be turned out as described in order to have the plane of the body angled towards the spectators. Otherwise a distortion in posture results which is most unnatural. But this cannot happen with the body held in an oblique posture, for one foot must turn out at an angle from the other foot.

Next allow me to explain the stage pace [*passus scenicus*]. For as all young men do not possess bodily agility, they must be given training in the appropriate methods of standing and walking on the stage. If perchance in explaining about the manner of treading the stage my description seems surprising, novel or affected, I hope the reader will prove not hasty and intolerant in his judgment of this practice.

I contend that the actor should adopt a particular and consistent pace when moving on the stage. The stage pace is consummated in a series of three or four steps that allows the actor to proceed in such a manner as to constantly preserve the proper turnout of the feet (the acting angel referred to previously). This technique should be observed scrupulously: let me explain how it is done. When an actor wishes to cross from one place on stage to another, his movement will be awkward unless he first withdraws the downstage foot slightly to the rear of the upstage foot. The forward foot, to repeat, is drawn back and again moved forward to a position beyond that which it had first held. The second foot is now advanced to a position beyond that originally held by the first, following which the first foot briskly steps out ahead of the second. In walking, the actor must constantly remember to keep his feet turned out. Thus, one leg takes the first step, the other leg the second step, the one the third and the other the fourth. Now the actor stands for a moment as if to stop. In order to advance further but without leaving the stage, the actor must execute a slight turn by drawing back the one leg at the fifth step and placing it slightly behind the other leg (still in the fourth step). Then the actor walks as before and assumes a standing position as before. Thereafter, with the position of the feet altered, he moves forwad again, as described initially. Thus he can preserve the acting angle and the required manner of walking which I designate the stage pace. I merely affirm what is common practice. The reader will pardon me if a verbal description seems less clear than an actual demonstration of this technique.

Perhaps some will declare this style to be too formal and affected— frivolous, superfluous nonsense invented by a fool, unworthy of the attention of a sensible person. To settle this line of argument, let me state unequivocally that an actor cannot appear graceful when on stage unless he does as I have described. The experience, judgment and truthfulness of expert authority corroborate my view. The practice has long been accepted and assiduously cultivated by the best actors. I confess that I have spent many laborious hours as a director perfecting this exercise, and I have drilled young performers as yet unskilled in the technique. The discerning person does not resist the truth but accepts it straightaway when it is revealed to him.

Truly, all who are expert in the art hold that the basic position of the feet for the stage is the acting angle, that is—the feet turned out diagonally. This is the point: the actor automatically should assume the acting angle with his feet as soon as he ceases walking. He then will not have to readjust them awkwardly to the proper stance a moment or so after he has finished his walk, a behavior characteristic of one who is unfamiliar or unpracticed in the technique. In practice, therefore, a reciprocal relationship exists between standing and walking; where one leaves off the other begins. Any casual movement of the feet over and beyond the stride previously described is extraneous, wasteful and incorrect because it is not conducive to the purpose of artful, natural action. For nothing in art is done without effect. This is the primary reason for my justification of appropriate technique for the stage. The wise reader may judge for himself whether I would fabricate a manner of walking on stage which is improper, and so leave myself open to serious criticism, or rather compose a work worthy of the most serious criticism, or rather compose a work worthy of the most serious study. My only concern in this regard is that my explanations are unclear, not that I have said something which is untrue.

It is then appropriate that the stage director should be thoroughly knowledgeable of the manner of moving on the stage. He must observe other performers, men of artistic excellence who are skilled in the ways of walking and standing so that he might follow their example in teaching these skills to others. It is not necessary to effect the foot positions of the dancing master for acting, however, although generally this form of training may prove useful to the stage performer. Often in this fashion young players have developed agility, sureness and coordination in their leg movements. But the manner of standing and walking appropriate to the dance should not be observed too stringently in performing as a player, unless one wishes to lose the resemblance to nature (and nature is the better teacher in this instance) and to destroy the correct way of walking by holding the feet in distorted postures.

At this point also we may describe how an actor should stand and walk when other actors are present on stage with him so as not to usurp a dominant position or move when he is not supposed to, thereby drawing too much attention to himself. The actor should use the same manner of walking when with others as he does when alone on stage, but be more constrained in his movements so as not to take up so much space. Of course, when completely alone, the performer has greater space in which to play. This is especially necessary when he must present deeply felt emotions. Indeed I am not the only one to insist upon a proper manner of holding the feet in the acting angle while standing and walking on stage. Older and more serious play directors have drawn the correct turnout of the feet with charcoal or chalk on the floor of the stage to teach ignorant young performers how to place their feet decorously and not in that slovenly fashion which would occur if they were left to their natural devices. Indeed it is not easy to walk artistically on stage. For everybody does not have an equal propensity for the art; rather learning to act is a long process. Yet should the stage director adopt the way of walking theatrically which I have described, he will discover how it will enhance the quality of stage movement, while if he does not, the effect will constantly be imperfect and unpolished.

CHAPTER V

CONCERNING THE ACTIONS OF THE KNEES AND HIPS AND THE TECHNIQUES OF BOWING AND SITTING

Now as we direct our attention from the feet to the knees, we note that correct stage posture demands that either the right or the left knee be bent slightly so that it projects forward slightly depending upon the performer's preference while standing. To obtain this position, it is necessary for the performer to draw his other leg back and slightly contract the muscles of his hips, so that the upper section of the body is bent somewhat forward and the weight of the body rests on the rear leg. Figure II furnishes some idea of my meaning, although the artist's sketch is not sufficiently accurate to convey the idea exactly. The drawing renders the actor with his back to the audience, a practice which the actor should not attempt on stage, but tolerated here to make visible the slightly bent position of the knee. Observe also the posture of the hips, as well as of the arms and of the fingers which will be discussed subsequently. The hips are the chief means of controlling the midsection in bending, twisting, contracting or stretching to form the various theatrical attitudes.

The shoulders must move in contrast to the action of the hips. These parts are so conjoined that when one moves the other responds reciprocally to ensure a nicety of posture of the body. Indeed this contrasting action of the hips and shoulders is more significant than is generally believed in contributing to the effectiveness of outstanding theatrical posture. Consider my words and put this principle into practice and the truth will be plainly evident in the development of properly deft bodily action. In this regard, I strongly urge the neophyte actor to keep this principle firmly in mind when attempting to make his initial bodily movements. He should also note that painting and sculpture, to which we have referred earlier, also make use of this same vital principle.

At this juncture it would seem pertinent to discuss the action of the legs in bending and in sitting. Bending the knees is an action that a player must frequently perform. In so doing he should first arrange his clothing so as not to offend against modesty in the eyes of the spectators. If female characters are employed (as indeed they must be) in a performance, they should kneel on both knees, which is more seemly for their sex than bending on one knee, a practice appropriate only for males.

Sitting should be done on a seat which will permit the actor's legs to reach the floor and not dangle in the air. The knees should be placed as much as possible in the manner I have already described for the standing posture. To permit this position to be taken most readily, the actor should sit on the front edge of the seat and not allow his entire weight to sink back onto the couch. The more easily the actor controls his body, the more deftly will he execute the action of sitting.

CHAPTER VI

CONCERNING THE ARMS, ELBOWS AND HANDS

Coming now to the actions of the arms, elbows and hands, we should bear in mind that the arms generally should be held away from the trunk in performance. They should move freely, but not touch the hips or sides or be overly extended or be placed before the head and chest. Figure I shows the weakness of having the elbows tucked too closely into the waist and not properly separated from the torso. Figure II shows the manner of extending gracefully the right arm while placing the left hand on the hips, which keeps the elbow away from the trunk. This principle is also evident in Figure III, as well as the principle that the arms should not be equally extended or exactly matched to each other in attitude. Rather one should be raised somewhat while the other is lowered, one slightly extended and straightened, the other slightly contracted and bent. But both should be well elevated with the elbows away from the body. This is the correct style of arranging the arms, a practice which can be observed in the work of knowledgeable painters and sculptors.

We should be especially careful to see that beginners keep the movements of their arms and hands away from the center line of the body, and not lower the hands below the waist but keep them raised. I say it should be chiefly inculcated in beginners because it is at this moment in their careers that they are crude in their actions, and, overcome with stage fright and nervousness, they dare not extend their arms. As a result, they invariably make gestures too closely to the belly, which is indecent and awkward, a violation of natural propriety. Unless young performers quickly unlearn this error, repetition will form it into a habit and they may never attain perfection in acting.

A more important reason for the adoption of this principle is that there is a natural impulse to raise the hands and arms to the upper level of the body when we behave energetically. For while we are talking forcefully to others we also make specific reference by gesture to what we are talking about. And this cannot be done unless we raise our arms and hands to gesticulate. In the same way, unless the performer trains his body to assume those graceful attitudes which are based on natural principles, he will never be able to act with that artistic rhythm [*eurhythmia*], and with the appropriate, decorous bodily movement which Cicero and Quintilian have identified.

There are other traditional rules which must be mentioned at this point. The arms should not be allowed to hang loose and uncontrolled, nor constantly swung back and forth as if preparing to hurl a javelin. As a general rule the right arm may extend somewhat, but not too far—only its own length, and then only when the gesture indicates some extraordinary circumstance. Generally the left hand does not move too much; on occasion it may be placed on the hip or share in some action with the right hand. However (except in the expression of some extreme passion), neither arm should be raised higher than the shoulders or the eyes.

About the hands: first it should be noted that the hand is a most effective instrument in acting when the wrist joining it to the arm is kept agile and loose. Secondly, the fingers should be arranged so that the index finger is kept fairly straight while the others curl increasingly and successively towards the palm. See Figure III. What I am trying to convey is that the fingers should not remain outstretched like sticks of wood, but that they should be bent in their own particular fashion, sometimes flexed more, sometimes less, sometimes fully extended, sometimes contracted according to propriety and the emotions to be rendered. I advice the neophyte to train his fingers assiduously to become deft and pliable, so that with all their expressive movements, they may contribute to the representation of a character.

At this point, let me digress briefly to answer the question as to whether actors ought to wear gloves on stage. Recently it has become fashionable to do so, although hitherto the great majority of players, unaware of the practice, did not do so. For more than fifty years as a spectator and play director in the theatre, I have never witnessed an actor wearing gloves while performing a role. Hence, these new-fangled actors have not changed my mind about the folly of this procedure. If I seriously challenge this novelty, I do so with the full force of ancient authority behind me. Unless it becomes a new custom for showing proper reverence for heads of state as part of court etiquette, I am dedicated to its future proscription from the theatre.

Moreover, theoretically and practically such a custom has no place on the stage because it essentially weakens and destroys the effectiveness of the hands. Whether occurring in nature or in art, effective communication demands that the hands be visible, especially if what is to be conveyed is of a delicate emotional tone. But this quality cannot be achieved if the hands are rendered inflexible by gloves or if the finger movements are indistinct because they are swathed in material. I do not speak spitefully in this fashion, but because I truly am convinced that wearing gloves on stage interferes with the actor's artistic effectiveness. The wise person knows that superficial finery can be used to cover unskillful movement and that such trickery is evidence of a lack of artistry. It would be as dishonest to mask the face, the seat of emotions, as to cover that fine acting instrument, the hands.

Then too, what would happen if the actor, as is often the case, must perform specific business with his fingers—opening, writing and signing letters, taking and counting coins from a purse and other such actions. If the hands were gloved all such actions would have to stop until the gloves were removed. The resulting delay would be theatrically inappropriate; it would be disturbing or ludicrous to the spectator if the business were not executed expeditiously. Wearing apparel of this type is a hindrance to artistic performance because it hinders natural function.

I do not grant that because actors in the theatres of court wear gloves that we must do the same. We need not follow the example of those who supervise court productions, who encourage their actors to behave with extravagance and exaggeration, even beyond the bounds of truthful action and decorous conduct, which is the rule that we follow. For the court drama is not deemed the cynosure of art. If a playwright uses it as a model his work will be ostracized by the critics and his play consigned to oblivion. I am not saying that same court performances are not praiseworthy, but that they are in error in appealing to the taste of the audience for spectacularity rather than in being guided by the sober rules of art. While the court theatre may be allowed its customary procedures, other theatres please through more modest circumstances. Hence, a stage in which the rules of nature and art are practiced, not for creating ostentatious effects, but for cultivating a sense of graciousness and for revealing the emotions, is perhaps a better place for the representation of verisimilitude according to the laws of art and nature.

However, while I do not generally allow gloves to be worn, I do not entirely reject the practice providing the actor is wearing contemporary German or French dress. Let him have a glove on his left hand only with the right hand bare while engaging in casual conversation, as in Figure IV. At least, this is less of an abuse, in my opinion. Others may decide the matter otherwise. Now back to my discussion of the action of the hands.

The action of the right hand is paramount in playing. Still I do not advise that the left hand be kept immobile, but that it aid the right in gesticulation when speech demands its use. At certain times, however, the left hand should be kept absolutely motionless while the right hand alone is used. When speaking about himself the actor may touch his breast or at least refer to himself with a gesture of the hand. I must again give warning not to raise the hands above eye level, lest in so doing they slip past to block the audience's view of the actor's eyes and face. The hands should not be thrust into the bosom or the pockets, etc. They should never be clenched into fists, unless, perhaps, rustics are to be portrayed who must exhibit boorish behavior. Of course, occasionally if great anger is to be portrayed, a threatening gesture can be produced by clenching the fists.

Ordinarily it is poor practice to clap the hands together so as to make a noise. Yet it is tolerable in farcical scenes as when children tease a fool or some such character. The practice of cracking the knuckles or snapping the fingers to show displeasure or contempt should not be completely banned, because, if discretely used, it reveals a quality of haughtiness or at least indignation. I am speaking here about portraying noble characters who must not seem vulgar or improper in their actions, but must possess an air of calmness and dignity. So say those who are knowledgeable about the amenities of stage performance.

There is the question of the extent to which action should correspond with speech. Consider whether or not the actions of wood-chopping, drawing a bow, shoveling earth, spear-throwing, and so on, should be imitated while speaking about them. Obviously it is more appropriate to make reference to them through words than by actual demonstration. This is especially so when it is easy to derive the meaning from the substance of the speech, for then to mimic the action would be blatant and ridiculous. Of course, gestures which are improper and indecent for public display should be avoided at all costs.

Quintilian in his *Institutio oratoria* (Book II, Chapter 3), Caussinus in his *Palace of Eloquence* (Book 9) and thereafter Voellus, Amadeus Bajocensis and others, have contributed substantially to the theory of hand and finger gesticulation. Let me present some of their ideas in abridged form:

1. Admiration is shown by raising both hands, but not past the upper most height of the chest, while turning the palms out to the audience.

2. Aversion is expressed by turning the face to the left side, away from the object of dislike, while both hands are directed to the

same object from opposite sides of the body and lifted slightly as if pushing the repellent object away. Similarly detestation is shown by only shaking the right hand slightly from the wrist, as if to drive away the distasteful object by this action.

3. Pleading is expressed either by raising the hands with the palms facing each other, or by lowering the hands with the fingers tightly intertwined.

4. Dolor or sadness is expressed by clasping the hands either at the height of the chest or at waist level. Giving testimony is conveyed by extending the right hand somewhat, and then bringing the hand to the breast.

5. An exclamation of surprise is made by swinging the arms decorously upwards with each hand somewhat open, the palms turned in slightly towards each other and also tipped back—by which the degree of surprise may be revealed.

6. Reproach is indicated by closing three fingers and leaving the index finger extended, or by closing the one or two middle fingers and leaving the others extended.

7. Encouragement is rendered by opening the arms and hands somewhat towards the person who is the center of attention, almost as if about to embrace him.

8. A question of doubt is indicated by raising the right hand with the palm turned out.

9. Repentance is indicated by placing the hand close to the breast.

10. Fear is conveyed by placing the right hand with the four fingers joined together and extended, on the breast, then dropping the hand allowing the fingers to relax.

In contrast to those gestures which are artistically contributive, there are others which detract from performance. These may be digested here:

1. It is artistically improper to extend the fingers so that they are overly separated from each other.

2. Also to join the tips of the thumb and fingers together, as in holding a pen when writing.

3. Also to keep the fingers stiffly extended and tightly pressed together when expressing deep emotion.

4. As previously mentioned, also to ball the hands into fists, except under extraordinary circumstances.

5. Also to rub, clean or inspect the hands, manicure the nails, or scratch the head or other parts of the body.

6. To gesticulate with the left hand alone is not approved.

7. It is boorish to indicate approval by much clapping of the hands.

8. It is artistically improper to repeat the same gesture and to make the same kind of movement over and over again.

9. It is artistically improper to raise the hands above the shoulders or the head, although a character who is severely afflicted or driven by the furies to a state of distraction may do so.

These rules, of course, are for beginners in the art of acting. The best guide is the rule of nature, to be free of affectation and to imitate the behavior of those whose comportment is deemed to be of excellent and praiseworthy quality.

CHAPTER VII

IN WHAT MANNER SHOULD THE OTHER BODILY PARTS, ESPECIALLY THE EYES AND HEAD, BE CONTROLLED TO ACHIEVE ARTISTRY IN PERFORMANCE?

The principal parts of man's body are his head and face which readily reveal his mental state. Consequently, the actor must always take pains to conform his features to what is indicated in the play script. In this respect the eyes are especially important, for in themselves they have the power to project effectively any expression otherwise revealed in the face. Often a wink of the eye at the right moment can prove more significant than a torrent of words. Therefore, the actor's first duty is to direct his eyes towards the audience and towards those on stage with whom he is conversing. But he should not stare fixedly at one or the other, but shift back and forth between the stage and the auditorium, as the performance dictates. The actor, however, should shift his attention so subtly as not to distract his audience. Used effectively the eyes can convey the affections most eloquently, even without the accompaniment of speech.

When the actor makes his entrance from the wings he should immediately turn his face and body towards the spectators and present his face in such a way that his eyes can easily be seen, for in them the audience may perceive his state of mind. Simultaneously, he must observe the correct manner of walking when on stage, and place his feet so that, while advancing, he can turn his face to his audience. We have drawn a sketch of this procedure in Figure V, but the artist's pen cannot catch precisely the action of the living player. Nevertheless, in this rough drawing, the reader may observe in some measure the action of the face, hands and feet. Let him note particularly in what direction these are facing while the actor's eyes are upon the spectators. For the actor's entire performance is dependent upon his being seen by the spectators and much depends upon the way in which he places his feet. The extended right hand with its slightly curled fingers indicates the actor to be a living human being, not an unbending man of stone.

Since the face and the eyes are universally believed to be the seat of the affections, the wise actor uses these parts to make manifest the emotions called for in the play, thereby evoking the emotions in the audience. For ordinary experience reminds us that the face and especially the eyes are extremely effective in revealing emotion. No further proof of this is needed than to remember that when love or joy is present the face does not wrinkle up but grows serene and happy; and so all emotions have their characteristic expressions.

Moreover, the eyes are so adept at this function that they may truly be said to be the seat of the affections. They are as outstanding in this regard as are the hands of a clock in indicating the hour, which cannot be known without the indicator, no matter how well shaped and beautifully colored the other parts. With his eyes the actor may most forcefully and efficaciously reach the hearts of those who watch him perform. A gentle expression conveys love, and intent look concentration, a serious glance fear, a stern appearance indignation, a sorrowful expression gloom. In a word, the eyes can be even more expressive than forceful speech.

I confess readily that just how these various expressions are to be formed cannot be explained so easily in words. Each person must privately apply himself to the problem, deciding according to his best judgment what is the best expression for each of the emotions. He should complete these studies prior to his rehearsing a part or performing in the theatre. Furthermore, he should carefully study the masterpieces of painting and sculpture as well as the actions of expert actors and even of preachers. By viewing such models he learns the correct images and so can imitate at will their external appearance by recalling their appearance in his mind. This piece of advice is particularly useful to those who lack a lively imagination, lest they be satisfied only with creating their own imagery. He who takes my advice seriously can testify as to how valuable is such an experience.

To proceed further: in conversation with others on stage the actor is enjoined to watch the one who is speaking. For if he does not do so he will be distracted and his features will prove unresponsive to what is transpiring. This fault is commonly encountered in boys who, when they first speak on stage, peer out at the audience and only begin to show expression when their cue comes to speak. How utterly ridiculous and how crude! The prudent actor always concentrated on his part so that the audience may perceive from his facial expressions and from his gestures what his responses are to the speeches of the other actors. Unless acting is sustained it becomes silly.

Therefore, the face and the entire chest should always be turned in the direction of the audience, for it is only proper that the actor be open to their gaze if the performance is for the audience's benefit. When the emotions grow in intensity it is all the more necessary that they be shown to the spectators. Only when the actor presents his face and body fully to the audience can his responses clearly be seen and impressed upon the audience.

I do not contend that the body not be allowed to turn to one side or another. On the contrary, the position of the body and of the feet which I have already described requires that a lateral position be assumed. But I truly believe that the actor should turn his face completely to the audience while holding his body obliquely in their direction. See the proper example I have furnished in Figure VI. Though here the actor affects sadness by standing with his hands clasped, he does not turn them or his body fully towards the spectators. Nevertheless he presents his face and aims his speech directly at them.

During a stage conversation, then, the speaking actor should take pains to direct his words at the audience and not at his fellow actor. While other gestures may be made in the direction of his listening partner, the play of the features should be presented to the audience. Of course, when the actor stops speaking he may direct his gaze at his partner again. The reason for this rule derives from the need of the audience to see and hear what is taking place on stage, for it is for the spectators that the theatre exists. But if actors were to converse among themselves and were to look at and address each other as though no spectators were present in the auditorium, then half the audience would be deprived of a front view of the talking actor and would be able only to catch a side or a rear view of him. Such a position is offensive on grounds of want of artistry and ordinary politeness, but especially because it prevents the spectators from seeing the actor completely, which is fundamental to the performance of the play. Moreover, the actor's very words cannot reach them, for, when sound is directed away from and not at the audience, its members remain unaware to a great degree of what the actor is saying. And when the audience can neither perceive the actor's emotional expression nor sufficiently comprehend his words, how indeed can they be responsive to the play? Hence, it is obvious that when the actor is speaking he is obliged to turn his head to the spectators, though he may direct his gestures and the position of the rest of his body at his fellow actors. Of course, upon completing a speech, the actor can then glance at the other stage performers. Let him not be deceived, however, into imitating the natural mode of conversation in which both parties continuously look at each other. For when two people discourse, both are speakers and auditors and do not have to address a third party. But on stage the matter is otherwise; the audience for whom the actor's speeches are intended is present. There is general agreement, notwithstanding, that the listening actor should respond to what the speaking actor is saying, even though he does not see the speaker's entire face. Figure VIII, *infra,* will clarify my meaning to some degree. Here I have drawn two positions in which an actor may stand while speaking. In both instances the face is directed at the audience, while the body is turned in the direction of the other actor. While this is an eminently suitable posture, it is not the only means of handling the business of speaking and listening. Other positions are mentioned in due course.

CHAPTER VIII

FURTHER OBSERVATIONS ON ACTING AND ESPECIALLY ON THE EMOTIONS

At this point let me advance some views about the techniques of acting which are generally acknowledged by experts in the field. One is that movement should precede speech, a principle which should be followed by students of performance. Before an actor answers the speech of another actor he should indicate overtly what he intends to say, responding in such a way that the audience can learn what his feelings are and can anticipate what his verbal responses will be. For example, if one actor should request something which the other actor will not or cannot supply, the second actor may reveal the fact that he is going to deny the request of the first by making a gesture of refusal even before speaking the actual words. The same holds true for other actions as well.

This principle is natural in origin. In the process of speaking, before words come to mind, the speaker may detect a natural internal reaction as to whether his response will be pleasant or unpleasant. The reason for this first response is that the body reacts more quickly to sensation than to reason. Moreover, it is easier to indicate meaning by gesture than by speech, since the mind must be more directly involved in speech than in gesture. In fact, the feelings are directly formed from the mental images [*phantasis*], while words first have to be constructed, as in a workshop, by the process of reason, into a linguistic form which can be understood when spoken aloud.

It is the same in nature. The flash of light reflected from two clashing cymbals strikes the eye before the sound reaches the ear. And similarly in man, perception initially takes place when a mental image stirs the feelings before reason brings expression to the emotions in the form of words. Hence the actor should follow nature's way of gesture preceding speech.

Another critical note I must make is about the actor who stops displaying emotion when he ceases speaking. Immediately thereafter his face goes blank and his eyes wander curiously over the audience.

(This is particularly notable among children.) Or, of the actor who, when his speech is over, abruptly alters his expression. (This is peculiar to inexpert performers.) Rather, the emotion should be continued for as long as there is need for it in the substance of the speech and only thereafter should it be allowed gradually to subside, and then until the moment when the actor must assume still another expression. My conclusion is that the mark of puerile or inexpert acting is allowing the features to be inexpressive except when speaking. Students, therefore, should be advised as to how the serious actor uses his eyes when speaking, and how he trains them to be responsive. This type of training is necessary especially for beginners, as frequent and early exercise can discipline the eyes in correct performance, while later training—after the candidate has already had stage experience—may produce laboriousness and hesitancy in their use. So acting teachers should instruct their students early how to acquire the habit of diligent practice in private so that later they may appear in public with a sense of security and confidence.

Now that I have commented critically on training methodology, let me digress once again to insert a brief word of advice to those who instruct young performers. Before beginning his career as a teacher of acting, the instructor himself ought to be thoroughly grounded in acting techniques. He then can consistently speak and move in the appropriate manner for his students. But if the instructor instead rashly undertakes to teach acting without adequate preparation, he will risk having his speech and actions vary from day to day. As a consequence, his pupils will always be at a loss to know the correct course of action to follow. They will always be nervous and unable to give generously of themselves, especially if they have incorporated into their own stage behavior those flaws which they have picked up from the performance of their inadequately prepared instructor. As a result, it is not uncommon to find students who are otherwise potentially competent actors lacking the courage to assume challenging parts after they have fallen into such an unfortunate state in their training.

Now that my digression on pedagogics is over, permit me to return to my subject—the eyes as an important means of displaying emotion. As was mentioned earlier, the actor may actually shed tears if he can do so artfully or naturally in order to reveal deep sorrow, contrition, or other heartfelt conditions. The business is all the more pleasurable to the audience if it can be accomplished without the impression of fakery. When speaking of the heavens it is appropriate to raise the eyes, and similarly to lower the eyes when talking of the earth. These actions are acceptable, providing that they are not done ungracefully, such as by leaning the head forward more than is becoming, or tipping it too far backward. In the latter case it may cause the belly to protrude, which is a serious error in posture.

I must make some additional comments on the rendering of the emotion of sadness. Frequently this is done by clasping the hands with the fingers intertwined, either at a level above or below the waist. In either case, care must be exercised to see that the clasped hands be held on the right or left side of the actor—whichever is more comfortable—but not held at the midline of the body. For if this were done the speaker's face might be blocked from the audience's view when he raises his hands—a technical error, since the actor must always keep his features open and visible to the spectators. Certainly decency does not sanction the hands being held too low. Figure VII nicely illustrates this action.

I shall add a few more words concerning the affections. First of all, the actor should make sure that he expresses the actions involved in the projection of deep thought (an emotional state found in most plays) with as much vivacity as is possible. Changing the body position, the walk and the gestures contributes in some measure to achieving the desired effect. For example, sometimes the actor can lean forward, apparently silently considering what he is going to say, what course he must take or decision he should reach. Sometimes he can stand erect with one hand placed on a nearby table, the other employed in gesticulation, the better to convey his passing thoughts. Sometimes also he can place an elbow on the table at which he is sitting, lean his head on his hand and soliloquize. Thus, by varying the attitudes of the body to conform to those of the mind, the actor can artistically and eloquently express himself to his audience.

Occasionally, in extreme sorrow or misery, the performer may quite properly cover his face with his two hands or bend over and bury his face in his arms. In the process he may murmer into his elbow or to a handkerchief. Though these few words are scarcely audible, their tone conveys the depth of the character's sorrow in a way in which distinctly articulated speech could not. However, this action should be of short duration lest it prove distasteful to the spectators.

So in enacting sorrow the player should make greater use of physical action than of speech. For this reason the words may be pronounced indistinctly, the flow of language interrupted with aposiopeses, broken off, split up, and produced with a heaviness of spirit—the true signs of melancholy. Frequently the effect of profound sorrow can be produced by remaining entirely mute, or by sighing slightly, or by giving vent to a brief exclamation. By all these means sorrow may be rendered and conveyed strikingly to the spectators. The reason I have chosen to talk about this particular emotion is that it produces a strong noticeable outward effect upon the body. Therefore, because this extraordinary passion causes a unique external manifestation by which an emotion can be recognized, in turn it can produce a similar reaction in the spectators when they see it produced before them by the actor.

The same reason holds for all other kinds of affections as well. The more glowing the performance of the actor, the stronger, more lively and powerful are the emotions felt by the spectators. For the senses are the gateway to the heart through which various ideas pass and, while in the seat of emotions, become agitated. These quickened impressions then can be seen on the surface of the body and thus serve theatrical purposes.

The presence of such emotions as joy, love, desire, etc., is recognizable by such expressions as copious discourse, gaiety, kissing and other lighthearted kinds of actions. Since these require no great skill to reproduce, I shall refrain from further comment.

Concerning the rendering of another kind of emotion, anger, I must provide a description. When this passion begins to agitate the heart, the forehead wrinkles, the lips compress, the pace quickens, and the hands and arms begin to move with increasing speed. Speech also becomes more rapid and interrupted, and marked by brief insertions and interjections. Subsequently, the angry person may directly attack the one who provoked his rage, if present; or if not, he may persist in heaping imprecations on the absent object of his fury, may gesticulate violently, snap his fingers and gnash his teeth. By such passionate activity anger is normally expressed. If anger becomes excessive and degenerates into violent fury, the actions of the body become equally immoderate, and a person in a fit of rage may commit unseemly and insane actions. Consequently, the prudent actor should constantly let his stage conduct remind us that there is a trace of dignity in all men, and especially in illustrious persons. Otherwise the stage would become Bedlam [*morotrophium*] instead of a center for teaching sagacity [*orchestra prudentiae*].

It is also unnecessary to demonstrate to the common manifestations in gesture and speech of the gentler emotions, as their appearance is easily discoverable from the general principles enunciated in the course of this essay.

CHAPTER IX

AN APPENDIX TO CERTAIN INFORMATION ON BODILY MOVEMENT MENTIONED EARLIER

They are indeed wise who have said that movement and gesture are the eloquence of the body.[4] For as the mind speaks through words, the body expresses what it feels through the actions of its members. For this reason the actor must be sure to know the natural movements of the body which correspond to the meaning of the words he must speak. Thus he can hope to display emotion pleasingly, provided he has correctly composed his actions according to the rules governing excellence in the art of acting, and not solely according to the dictates of his rude nature.

Indeed to do so he must be exceedingly careful to suit all gesture to its appropriate speech and corresponding thought, without an affectation or archness of manner which may prove offensive to his audience and so destroy the favor that the actor is seeking.

Since the beginning and end of acting is to stir the audience's emotions in the manner planned by the stage director, it is generally necessary for the actor to know exactly what the playwright had in mind, to set this same meaning in his mind and express it vigorously and simultaneously in words and actions. The talent of the performer should be of a kind that, if perchance the director has not succeeded in creating fine dialogue, the actor, by the excellence of his technique, can remedy this discrepancy and make the action pleasing.

Still another critical point concerning body movement must now be made. The actor should not move all the time, but should stop when he finishes speaking. Then when he begins to speak again he should add suitable actions to the new material. Perhaps he could move his head while making an assertion or denial, or while replying to a colleague. The performer should make his actions especially vigorous when displaying the affections of indignation, anger, or other violent passions.

What is the correct position for actors engaged in conversing on stage if indeed the face must be presented entirely to the audience, as was previously discussed? And when more than two actors are present does this not create an even greater problem? Under other circumstances, it would seem perfectly natural to have the conversationalists face each other.

I have an answer to this double question. First, the action of the hands, as well as the other movements of the body, should be directed at the listening actor. But, at least during the time when he is talking, the speaking actor should turn his face and direct his speech at the audience. Second, the other actor who is preparing to speak should face his companion to allow the latter to observe his features. Thus the listening actor will not be totally deprived of the effect of the appearance and the sense of the words of the speaking actor, and so can readily anticipate what will be said. I have already made a brief reference to Figure VIII in Chapter VII. This illustration of two possible positions for the speaking actor indicates quite nicely what I am trying to make clear. Here we see an actor directing his gestures and the position of his body to a companion, while keeping his eyes and face open to the audience.

CHAPTER X

ON DELIVERY

Delivery [*Pronuntiatio*] and action [*Actio*] are nearly synonymous. So Soarius teaches, based on Cicero and Quintilian, that *delivery* is said by many to be *action*, although the latter properly refers to the gesture of the body and the former to the enunciation of words by the voice.[5] Though delivery and action are a single entity, yet they may be divided into two parts according to the manner in which they affect the senses. Delivery affects the soul through the ear, while action does the same through the eye. Since gesture has been previously treated, we shall now turn our attention to the voice and thereafter to delivery.

The prime characteristic of fine delivery is that it must be natural. This is to say that the actor must not speak his lines in a manner other than that spoken in familiar discourse among men of quality. The only difference is that the voice must be somewhat louder and more resonant to reach a large and distance audience.

Father Juventius S.J., also wisely makes this suggestion in his program for learning and teaching declamation for young men. In his declamatory exercises he advises that speech be low at first, as if explaining something in a natural manner to a friend, and that this style be used in formal delivery. The first concern of the actor is to know thoroughly the meaning of what he must recite. And so he should render into the vernacular with great pains what he will later declaim in Latin speech. For when the actor learns the meaning underlying the words he will understand how to use vocal intonation in a natural manner of expression. At the same time, other experts in delivery should regularly be brought before the students so that examples of proper usage may be demonstrated, since practitioners are more apt at showing these techniques than is the relatively unpracticed instructor.

Another characteristic of fine delivery occurs when vocal expression accords with the meaning of the words and the audience is touched by emotion as a result. To this end—that delivery should possess an emotional quality—the actor must first allow his own spirit to be moved thereby moving his audience. For how can anyone who is emotionally frozen warm others?

In this regard care should be exercised to see that vocal delivery does not stay the same. Instead, as reason and nature dictate, the voice at one moment should be intense, at the next relaxed, now loud, now soft, now rapid, now slow.[6] Each emotion in man has its characteristic vocal pattern. By mastery of his art the actor can achieve control of these tonal effects.

Consequently, attention must be paid to see that each vocal modulation corresponds to its appropriate emotional pattern. Thus love requires a tender, passionate manner of speaking, hate a harsh and severe one, joy a gay and excited tone, sorrow a broken tone interrupted by querulous sighs, fear a tremulous hesitant tone, audacity a bold and contentious speech manner, anger an impetuous and precipitate tone of voice, contempt an inconstant and somewhat ridiculing quality, a tone of amazement—half-spoken and half-silent and querulousness a complaining, pitiable way of speaking.

Indeed sterile language cannot reasonably explain how to teach vocal expression just as it cannot explain the postures of the body, although the latter can at least be indicated in drawings. We therefore must put greater reliance upon ear training to correct weakness in delivery. One such weakness is monotony—the same even tone without variation—certainly an egregious torture to an audience.[7] The same weakness is evident in the lay-preacher who reads his sermon from a book and pronounces every word with equal force or uses the same accentuation for every sentence. The delivery of the voice should be more flexible, sometimes raised, sometimes lowered, sometimes more rapid, sometimes more deliberate.

However, the actor should be careful not to fall into a singing pattern which allows too much tonal variation in the voice. He should also take pains not to allow the voice to fall too precipitously from an extremely high to an extremely low pitch without making use of intermediate voice levels. For the repetition of a high to low inflectional sequence is also a weakness, although the opposite of monotony. The actor who is unaware of the need to vary his tone in accordance with the meaning of the words is also in grave error, inasmuch as he cries out too vigorously when the word sense dictates that he should talk quietly, and talks too quietly when the word sense dictates that he should cry out vigorously.

The teacher should be careful not to allow the voice of a youngster to crack at an inopportune moment, or his student to say too many words uninterrupted by a breath. The student should know how to observe the punctuation marks, the stopping places for speech. He should not heedlessly neglect the virgules and commas which are check points in the speech flow. The major stopping places, the periods, are like stations on a highway. They allow a pause to be taken for the length of time needed to regain breath and to obtain one's location. Some people while reciting hexameter commit the error of coming to a complete halt regularly at the end of each line, or, in declaiming pentameter, stop in the middle or before each disyllabic word, to make a caesura, by which means a short verse is usually terminated.

Rather this principle should be followed: continue the voice to the point where the meaning is complete, unless perchance the combination of words is so extensive that it cannot be expressed in one breath. In this case a brief pause may be taken at some midpoint. This will not be wrong if, upon completion of the sentence, the pitch of the voice is placed well below that of the pitch taken at the intermediate stopping point. But the actor should be extremely careful to see that the final sounds before a pause for breath are distinctly heard. For the fading of the voice is wont to happen with a consequent loss in meaning.

And now, at the request of those who are play makers, I shall discuss briefly the stage, playwriting and dramatic art, and so disclose what toil, study and experience have taught me about these subjects. My explanation follows.

CHAPTER XI

CONCERNING SUPPLEMENTARY AIDS TO PLAYWRITING AND TO DRAMATIC ART

These are the qualities I demand in a theatre director. Besides talent, without which nothing can be accomplished, he first of all should be a playwright and a Latinist, be strongly imaginative and creative, possess a thorough knowledge of human behavior [*sit egregius Ethicus*], be known as an actor, and finally, have a basic knowledge of the manual arts.

These are requisites for success in the theatre. But if the director were also an expert in music and in painting (which I would hope for but not expect), he would merit all possible applause. I shall discuss each of these qualities separately.

He should be a playwright so that he may know the ancient laws governing artistry. He should be endowed with poetic ingenuity to devise clever peripetys and turns of events, which make comedy and tragedy pleasant and enjoyable.

He should be a Latinist lest he prove crude in his diction and unrefined in his idiom, and so that he may conform his speaking style to the emotions which he wishes to make his audience feel.

He ought to have a vivid imagination to create theatrical characters, actions and effects, without which a performance is weak, confused, and poorly put together. The more vigorous the director's talent, the more powerful in his production.

He should also have a knowledge of human behavior, so that he may know what the emotions are, from whence they arise, by what means they are provoked, sustained and dissipated. He also should be informed as to how emotional reactions are inhibited so that he may remove such impediments. In a word, he should know how to excite and maintain emotional effects—the very heart of his work.

The director should be an actor, versed in the rules of acting as was developed hitherto. He should not merely know them but teach them by his own example.

Let me say this about having a knowledge of the manual arts. There are some people who are so capable at manual craftsmanship that they can make anything which they can see, or imagine in their minds. They are of great assistance in the theatre, for they know how to turn everything in their own use and how to make something out of nothing. Other people are not able to make anything with their hands, yet they can grasp the construction of a design and inform others how to make it. For instance, they are aware of what is significant in painting a picture—how to model the human body, to intensify and subdue light and shade, to divide space proportionately, to handle the details of character, of costume and of scenic background, to manage perspective illusion, and to deal competently with many other specific items which they must know about, even if they cannot directly express such information with a paintbrush. There are still other people who know nothing at all about design. They are ingenuous and simple folk, able to hammer a nail or saw wood. But they lack the ability to see these actions in their minds, or to explain how these actions should be performed to others. Hence, it not infrequently happens that if ordinary workmen are assigned to a task involving the direction of others, they may not be able to fulfill the assignment properly, with consequent loss of money and effort. Certainly they are deprived, under the circumstances, of any satisfaction which comes ordinarily from completing a piece of work successfully. For they cannot lead or manage others when they lack the innate ability to explain the operations involved in a piece of labor and to supply appropriate guidance.

The successful director should not hesitate to ask how something is done, lest its construction prove needlessly expensive, take too much effort, and be inopportune, unrelated and out of keeping with the play setting. Furthermore, if any person (and not a few are found) thinks that it is undignified for a literary man to be concerned with the manual arts or believes it sufficient to work in his study while composing a play solely according to the rules of art in which he considers himself expert, he should, in my opinion, leave the theatre and sound off from an academic chair; there he may attract more applause than in the theatre.

CHAPTER XII

OF THEATRICAL ART ESPECIALLY DIALOGUE

I confess my foolhardiness in daring to present my views on theatrical art, an area which is fraught with many subtle difficulties, in the opinion of learned men. I only offer my views because over the years I have labored to acquire some knowledge of the fine art of producing plays of all kinds. In spite of this long experience I still feel that I have insufficient knowledge to furnish complete instruction. Rather it is the spectators who insist that I tell them what I know about theatrical art. They are the ones who have applauded my presentations in the theatre on many an occasion. Certainly they did not come there merely to flatter my vanity or to see whether I was using the proper rules of theatrical composition.

Of course, it may be argued that spectators all too often praise the most banal and awkward dramatic writing for which true connoisseurs would not give a penny. Ordinary playgoers are inclined to enjoy only ludicrous action or lavish scenic display. But about the true art of dramatic construction—the plotting of the story, the invention of a suitable theme, the styling of the language, the development of the behavior and actions of the various characters, and other such pertinent and essential details—they know nothing at all. For responding to an emotion in a theatre does not necessarily provide an audience with an understanding of the sources of that emotion, the means by which it was created or the principles of emotional behavior in general. And can a person who has little or no knowledge of performance be qualified to judge the work of one who professes some competence in theatrical matters?

To add to the problem, even those who are expert in the field are diverse in their opinions as to what makes for an effective performance. In point of fact, there is no art or science which is so prone to disputation as is humane letters, particularly playwriting. The average person who listens to a theological or philosophical debate marvels at the ability of the discussants to argue so complicated a subject, and so refrains from stating his own lay opinion. Similarly there is little conflict of opinion about the principles of mechanics, for so few understand them. But the Muses speak a universal language. Nearly everyone has an opinion about artistic matters; it is in one's very nature to do so. Whoever thinks he has found the perfect method in art also discovers something which does not fit into his system. He thereupon must label that which lies outside his well-regulated program as unnatural, a distortion of art. And so there develops so much contradictory advice, conflicting opinion, calumny, arbitrary pronouncements, insults and derision.

Just to recall how experts can bicker among themselves is tiresome—how one sticks rigidly to the rules and models of the ancients; how a second turns his back on precedent and feels himself at liberty to create for his own day; while a third steers a course midway between the two. What one approves, the other disapproves, and thus they exchange opinions back and forth and take issue with each other.

To remember the details of their positions is also impossible. When it comes to style there are as many battles as there are authors. One is dedicated to meter in playmaking and proscribes prose. Another uses prose to make his language more comprehensible and so rejects verse. A few believe that both can be used effectively on stage. If one allows the presence of nonmetered but elevated prose in his dramatic writing, he is censured for being grandiloquent and a poet who cannot write poetry. If another writes plainly his style is condemned as gross. If he omits a word from the ancient quotation the critics pick at him like carrion crows. But the most lavish in their criticism are those who have never had practical theatrical experience, but who only may have read something about playwriting in a book. These types carp freely at everything and are the most disgusting and deadly for a playwright to encounter.

The great number of these critics have made me reluctant to expose myself as a target for their poisoned arrows. Yet, for the sake of those who need assistance in dramatic writing, I shall modestly venture to offer some useful, but not authoritative advice on the subject.

Initially we need to recognize the number and kind of plays or performances which are regularly found upon our stage. These are, in addition to the dialogue (or to put it incorrectly—declamation), drama, comedy and tragedy. Let us examine them individually.

The dialogue is the simplest form, in which two or more performers converse with each other about any subject. It lacks a plot or emotional characterization. The preparatory training exercises [*progymnasmata*] of Pontanus, and similar material belong in this category.

I am of the opinion that this should be the first exercise to be assigned to the playwriting student. At this point in his career he needs to learn the distinctive nature of the dialogue form, its style, diction and manner. For it may be written to be declaimed in an oratorical fashion, to be chanted poetically, or to be spoken in familiar conversation. Yet even the last, the colloquial style, borrows something from the previous two. From the study of declamation comes a concern for the meaning of words as well as a sense of style. From the study of poetry comes facility in making ingenious turns of phrase, in ornamenting a composition and elegance in language, besides a knowledge of metrical form. The informal colloquy demands a style which is succinct, informed with bright remarks and studded with erudition, aphorism, and similar figures of speech, especially when the characters involved in the conversation are of elevated rank. Those of lesser social pretension, however, should be made to use a cruder sort of diction which is the mark of lower class speech.

I have declared the dialogue to be devoid of a regular plot, although it is an essential ingredient of tragedy or comedy. Both of these forms make use of intricate deceptions and clever turns of events, with accompanying emotional effects. The dialogue does not require these elements. Rather it consists of a clear and straightforward argumentative conversation, sometimes treated seriously, sometimes humorously. Any display of emotion which becomes evident is purely accidental and without design.

Therefore, if anyone wishes to prepare himself to be a playwright, he should begin to exercise his talents in this easy medium before attempting more demanding forms. The simple dialogue can provide an illuminating test of a person's capabilities as a dramatic writer more than is generally realized. The student who makes use of it as a training vehicle can discover the many varieties of human personality, how men behave, how to argue wisely and skillfully, and what the objectives and methods are of dialogizing speech, the words to be employed and their arrangment. Without prior experimentation, all these matters cannot be acquired which are subsequently put into practice in the composition of larger dramatic works.

If anyone rashly omits this preliminary step in the training process and goes immediately to writing a major theatrical piece, he will be beset by difficulties the like of which he had never dreamed existed. For he will have to face problems of characterization, language usage, poetic measure, style and other basic concerns which stem from inadequate elementary training. He will become a butt for laughter and ridicule. Hence, that precocity or ardor which impels the young playwright to failure should be held in check. I refer here specifically to that lack of discretion and to that presumption which make immature writers overly dependent on their innate abilities, as well as to the desire for immediate success. As a result, without fundamental technique, they plunge into the writing of long and involved dramas; they impetuously don the sock and buskin before they are even ready to remove their ordinary shoes. Once, when they were young and impressionable, they saw a play which deeply affected them. Now, inspired by that earlier event, they are absolutely itching to produce that same effect in others; they imagine that just because they once have seen a play, they know all there is to know about playwriting. Naturally they have such an ambition before they know quite exactly what playwrighting is and what principles need to be mastered to obtain success in that art. It is the height of folly to plunge into deep water without some kind of float to buoy you up if you do not know how to swim! It is painful for me to recall the vast numbers of plays that I have seen which were failures simply because they lacked the simplest principles of theatrical composition. Nothing can be achieved but in its appointed time. To win, a racer must begin at the starting mark before gaining the finish line. It is not a disgrace to begin one's career as a humble student at the foot of Helicon, that mount of the Muses. After all, David was first a herder of sheep before he became a leader of men.

The study of simple forms of characterization has further utility for both teacher and student. It is now expedient for the teacher to demonstrate vocal inflection, articulation, gesticulation, and other basic performance techniques by means of relatively uncomplicated roles which are manageable by beginning students? Hence instructors can themselves memorize the dialogues of Pontanus and demonstrate the form in actual performance for their students to copy—a practice which I deem most worthy of praise.

Since the giving of declamations in public as a teaching exercise has the same purpose as that of dialogues, it would be splendid if the dialogue could be used as a scholarly pursuit on a par with declamation! For a dialogue well furnished with authoritative statements can substitute for a formal lecture on the subject.

CHAPTER XIII

OF DRAMA IN GENERAL

After the student has become sufficiently experienced in these first attempts at writing a play and the Muses have favored his efforts, he may proceed directly to formal dramatic composition. The word drama is a generic term which encompasses all types of theatrical writing including tragedy and comedy. But it is also a distinct form which is shorter and lacks the extensive division into parts which formal comedy and tragedy properly require. Therefore drama allows all that is employed in comedy and tragedy—theme, story, episodes, emotions, verse, music and other such items. But drama differs quantitatively from these classic forms in that it is shorter and its plot is different from that of tragedy or comedy, and it does not conform to all their laws or keep within their narrow thematic confines. Though I am speaking here of drama in the narrow sense, I acknowledge that many of the universal laws peculiar to tragedy and comedy are also applicable to this form.

However, I forebear to list here all the ancient laws posited for dramatic writing in general, first because they can be obtained from Father Maurus' excellent commentary on Aristotle, and second, because they have been carefully explained in many other authoritative works. Among these are Alexander Donatus' treatise on poetic art, Martin Du Cygne's on the same subject, Bohuslaus Balbinus' *Verisimilia*, and many others. I merely offer my views because of a long and personal involvement in the theatre.

As a first step the author of a drama should select a plot compatible with his own creative powers, appropriate to the background and characters he has chosen, and at the same time within the artistic capabilities of the performers who are at his disposal. If he does so he is likely to merit the applause of a discerning audience. Then he should separate his plot into its appropriate acts and scenes as he prepares an outline of the entire work before commencing the writing of the dialogue. In the selection of his materials he should be governed by the principle that what occurs on stage should seem to be actually taking place, and not make the mistake of becoming too involved in the petty details of a story. To this end he should eliminate and retain material on the strength of whether or not it stimulates feeling and edifies the audience. In this way he will be more subject to the requirements of art and can judge his work according to its own inner consistency and not according to whether or not it accords with actual fact. Now he must meticulously, and with the utmost concentration as in laying out a target range, set out the emotional effects needed for his theme, noting the moments where they emerge and vanish. At this point he needs to eliminate any emotion which is not absolutely indispensable and in accord with the tone of the play. Thereupon the playwright should test the effects of the play upon himself, assessing what is purely a personal reaction and what can be supported by the general laws of rhetoric, before inviting an audience's response. He should not just accept what he has written, but think long and hard about its erudition, its inventiveness and its capacity for arousing emotion, which give it dimension. He should consult Aristotle's *Rhetoric* in Father Maurus' commentary to discover the general principles underlying the excitation of the emotions, and how to put these principles into practice in the particular circumstances of a dramatic composition.[8] In this respect he should study how historic events may be adapted to play form, or how a clever tale by its very likeliness may become the basis for a stage play.

When I use the term stage play [*fabula comica*], I do not refer to an entirely new category of theatrical composition, but an already established dramatic form, like that of tragedy and comedy, which must subscribe to poetic invention—that is, which has plot complications, peripetys and actions.

This kind of play was so designated by ancient as well as modern writers, by which they meant an imperfect dramatic form unlike those which are so complete that nothing can be added or subtracted without spoiling the dramatic quality. For drama, tragedy and comedy are poetically complete within themselves, as well as being constructed of clever scenes and of actions linked by cause-and-effect relationship. To create an action which is only lifelike is insufficient. The unexpected as well as the truthful event must also be supplied. This is the pleasant, agreeable, and efficacious way in which an audience is kept in a delightful state of suspense. And if a sense of loving kindness can be inspired (the primary purpose of the Christian playwright), as well as that of honor and virtue, then there will be a great spiritual harvest.

Accordingly, the playwright must first execute the design of the stage play in his mind before committing it to paper. Then he should

Despite the fact that some believe this problem is not capable of solution, I do now modestly propose to try with the help of reason and authority to support my argument. We should admit that tragedy does not have to have a sad ending, nor exclusively concern a noble person who is cast down into wretched circumstances. We ought to ascertain from the study of the writings of the ancients that public plays were first devised to divert the attention of the populace by means of comedy, or in order to have them understand the horrible consequences of evildoing by viewing these unfortunate events presented in the form of tragedy. As a result of these entertainments the state could peacefully exercise its sovereignity. For wise rulers were of the opinion that the two most effective means of making men dutiful were through affection and dread. They produced the first by plays whose purpose was to inspire mirth, and the second by plays concerned with tragic events. Affection, they believed, could be induced by staging spectacles delighting the spectators and making them grateful to their leaders for the entertainment which they provided. Fear they sought to arouse by showing the terrible consequences of wickedness. The first became comedy, the second developed into tragedy.

Many men of talent have devoted themselves to formulating the precise rules by which a playwright could create a successful tragedy or comedy, in accordance with accepted standards of nature and art. They further sought to define the exact bounds of freedom to be allowed the playwright in delineating characters and situations. Earlier generations have left us a copious store of prescriptions designed to enhance the theatre of their own day, which their playwrights freely could utilize to make their own writing more artful.

But today times and customs have changed; so also have the goals and modes of theatrical presentation. Now we have theatres which provide uplifting entertainment, performed not before the vulgar mob, but before men of refinement and rank who are above coarse jests. The very idea of assaulting the sensibilities of a modern audience with old-fashioned tripe is unworthy and contemptible. Consequently, our modern playwrights do not have to be strictly concerned with meeting the conditions hitherto imposed with regard to the social rank of their leading characters, but rather to be able to please, edify and inspire a cultivated audience.

Nevertheless, a modern playwright, more often than not, will introduce deeply disturbing events into the otherwise happy life of a man of illustrious birth in order to correct evil action and so to provide an excellent example of the consequences of wrong-doing to the public (which is Aristotle's purpose). Or, if the example has consequences which are enormously evil, the playwright can achieve a successful response by making the catastrophe end in death, even if the wrongdoing of the protagonist and the consequent emotional responses do not occur as mandated by Aristotle.

By way of example of this sort of problem—suppose a playwright wishes to dramatize the coronation of a Rudolph or the wedding of a Theodosius, or the birthday of a Charlemagne, or of the pious actions of a Josephat, and a Calabytes (at this point I do not wish to introduce the use of martyrs as play subjects), or the lives of other men of faith and courage whose actions are, especially in their outcome, far removed from the conditions of sadness or death imposed by the ancient writers on tragedy. What should the modern playwright do if he wishes to conform strictly to Aristotelian regulation? Should he force his play into the narrow compass demanded by the ancients? Or should he totally abandon the old ideas? Arguments can be found on the part of academicians and those having but little knowledge to support both positions. But it is as unfortunate for experts to say that unless a play is constructed according to certain forms it is inexpertly constructed, as it is for those who wish to toss away Aristotle and the basic notions of the ancients and to declare that just because a play conforms to the rules it is boring and uninteresting.

What reconciliation is there in this struggle between one age and another and among men of conflicting opinions? If my description of this state of theatrical affairs is accurate, then this argument cannot be settled easily. But I do think on the one hand, that present-day playwrights might try to moderate their viewpoint (which is that plays should derive solely from the artistic taste of their own times) and might take the position that, when possible, the old forms should be employed. On the other hand, I believe that modern playwrights should be given considerably more latitude than is granted them by the ancient rules. I predicate this belief on the fact that the ancients themselves did not exactly follow their own precepts in all cases, and sometimes not at all. A perusal of ancient tragedy and comedy immediately reveals the concessions permitted in the social status of the leading character, his falling into error, and the liberties taken with the plot— even altering the endings of well-known stories, not to speak of the inability of the ancient playwrights to keep within the bounds of a single time span or locale. Recent playwrights should also be given greater freedom to adapt themselves to new theatrical conditions because times, customs and tastes change. Not a few learned men whose work has won highest praise and been approved by all have done so. Certainly we today should not possess the plays of Bidermann (with all their literary flaws!) if they had been judged solely according to the ancient standards. I do not wish to imply that the judging of works according to some critical standard is wrong, but that I support what [an unnamed] critic of reputation has said in defense of Bidermann (whom he calls a distinguished playwright) in an introduction to the printed edition of Bidermann's plays:

> What has Bidermann written which is reprehensible, unless it is that his work stands out from run-of-the-mill plays? Everyone knows how excellent his poetry is, and that he has been acclaimed for his playwriting. Only now, in his later years, after he has matured in his taste and become more expert in his knowledge as a result of experience does he venture to modify those rules of play-making (which were not always so closely observed by expert theatre practitioners of the past) and adapt them to suit the spirit of his own age, etc., etc.[10]

And further on:

> What can I say? That Bidermann is absolutely ignorant of the secrets of his craft, and that these secrets are known only to his critics? Or, dear reader, would you rather believe tht he has deliberately and intentionally tried to deal with the problem of reaching a well-bred contemporary audience etc.[11]

> Remember Father Bidermann is one of a number of playwrights of our order who writes on religious themes, whose works may be studied less for pleasure than for profit. These writers lure the souls of the spectators to virtue and to fear of God by depicting the actions of virtuous men in a pleasurable way. They know that applause will follow only if they are skilled in their art, etc. etc.[12]

> Our playwright has written for various types of audiences and given pleasure and profit to them all. Everyone is agreed that he arouses a love of righteousness in those who watch his plays. Indeed our author fully understands that spectators may be more effectively chastened by a play than by a sermon. As a final point, would his plays have had such an effect upon his audience if he had concentrated on keeping within the bounds prescribed by tradition, rather than devoting all the force and power of his talent to moving his audience? Instead he chose to disregard the views of a few critics, while still accepting the standards of the most learned.[13]

So reads the preface to Bidermann's plays.

I am not convinced that the form of a play must be purely original with the playwright, nor do I concede that he must totally forego the precepts of the ancient dramatic theorists. For the experience of generations and sound and reasonable judgment attest to the validity and correctness of the old principles to the extent that no doubt can exist as to the propriety of imitating nature (the cardinal principle), and the wisdom of achieving verisimilitude. I only insist (with apologies to the academicians) that a modern tragedy should not be censured if the requirements which the ancients imposed upon the protagonist are not strictly followed. For example, the playwright may substitute for the tragic flaw which causes the protagonist's terrible downfall, a flaw of another kind which does not precipitate so wretched a consequence. Similarly in comedy the playwright can allow a private individual engaged in his own affairs to fall into a miserable state. Other examples of this kind could be mentioned. If this concession were not allowed, the theatre would be shut to any playwright who did not exactly conform to the poetic regulation demanded by the learned. So a dramatist could not provide pleasant diversion for decent spectators because in his writing he was restrained by the severity of antique laws which for reasons aforementioned should be done away with. I have therefore come to the conclusion that the matter should be left to the playwright's discretion as to how far and exactly where he wishes to depart from classic precedent in tragedy.

If what I state seems too bold, let me assert that Father Donatus of our Order supports this position also. For in his discussion of the third requirement for characters of tragedy in the supplement to Chapter 11, Book 2 of his *Art of Poesy*, he clearly demonstrates the infrequency with which this stipulation was fully observed by the ancients:

> Why, therefore, did Aristotle formulate precepts and cite examples in a random fasion in the course of his writings, and why do we impose his laws upon our tragic playwrights if these laws are really useless?

Donatus answers his own questions:

> A law is not unfairly imposed if it can produce a play of outstanding quality, and can create beautifully finished characters. Examples do not always have to be found for each precept, especially if they are readily apparent, as they were for the Greeks in Aristotle's day. This greatest formulator of tragic principles took specific instances of poetic form from whatever tragedy suited his purpose. Since then his formal teachings have been difficult to follow.[14]

Through this quotation Donatus reveals himself as an exceptionally perceptive interpreter of Aristotle. A tragedy having a protagonist, though not completely and in all respects conforming to the Aristotelian model, is still a tragedy. If imperfect in this regard, it nevertheless should be called so because it has its own standard of perfection. Such a dramatic form may even be thought to be superior to the Aristotelian, since it involves an illustrious protagonist whose actions do not necessarily have to end in sadness and misery, but may continue on a felicitous course to the end. Yet, even if we grant the tragedy which omits the doleful ending to be a superior play form, it still must contain a variety of desperate and climactic situations. For unless the audience feels difficulty and danger, horror and anxiety, it really cannot enjoy a subsequent fortunate outcome.

Father LeJay, my contemporary, supports my view in his excellent statement:

Whosoever believes that a happy ending should be proscribed from tragedy must also condemn the tragedies of a goodly number of the ancient playwrights, particularly Euripides. For it is obvious that Aristotle was satisfied to have tragedy present the appearance of sorrow and trouble without having the stage run red with the blood of its victims. He still granted to playwrights the right to diverge from the regular rules to please an audience which is inclined by nature to be fickle and variable and hence to favor a happy conclusion. Indeed he believed that the distinction between tragedy and comedy lay in the sad ending for the former and the happy ending for the latter. But the bloody spectacles of tragedy were enjoyed by the ancients who were used to brutality, and consequently did not particularly distinguish between one form and another, except that tragedy had a more cruel climax. Today, however, we shrink from such bloody customs and believe that there is nothing wrong in presenting as a tragedy a play in which calamity turns out well. We are satisfied to demand that the plot concern the actions of illustrious men as they face danger, and nothing more.[15]

In addition, I am supported in my view by another authority, that of no less Father Joseph Juventius, the celebrated literary figure, author of *The Traditional Course of Education and Instruction for Teachers of the Society of Jesus* [*Ratio discendi et docendi Magistris Scholarum Societatis Jesu tradita*], who writes:

Tragedy is a dramatic poem revealing an action of some illustrious person. If this imitative dramatic action is noble in quality and the character of the person truly illustrious, the play is called a tragedy. If the action is ordinary, concerned with the business of common folk, the play is termed a comedy.[16]

Surely these remarks do not follow the precepts of Aristotle for tragedy and comedy very closely. For Aristotle requires additional conditions when he asserts:

> Tragedy is an imitation of an action which is illustrious, complete and of magnitude, in agreeable language and divided into several different parts, performed as a play and not narrated, which, through pity and terror, results in a purgation of such deep passions.[17]

Thus it is if we follow Aristotle and his ancient disciples. Tragedy demands, among other things, a purgation through pity and fear of similar profound and harmful emotions that originate in the human heart; that we are natually moved to feelings of pity and fear when we observe the awful calamities into which illustrious men have fallen through no fault of their own; that we learn to endure our own troubles more easily by feeling compassion for the troubles of others which are more serious than our own; and that we should fear and dread evil because it can fall upon us whether we deserve it or not. In contrast to Aristotle's definition, Father Juventius ignores the emotional concomitants of tragedy and is satisfied to have it be concerned only with the actions of an illustrious person. In Chapter 5, page 71, of his *Ratio discendi et docendi* he declares:

> Tragedy developed from the need to chastise princes and heroes, while comedy was instituted to teach ordinary men through examples drawn from domestic daily life. While a distinction is made between person and actions which are noble or ordinary, it is not from this source that the false notion derives that what ends dolefully is a tragedy and joyously a comedy. For do not many tragedies by Greek playwrights (who were certainly knowledgeable as to the rules) conclude on a note of joy and gladness? Hence tragedy should be restricted to imitating the actions of a noble person and comedy to imitating ordinary actions, though the principal figure does not have to be of humble rank. For in a dramatic poem action is the prime consideration, and has greater importance than the chief character. We are amply supplied with examples of action for imitation, but we are not supposed

to imitate the leading figure—only the quality of his actions. In point of fact, happiness is the ultimate goal of dramatic imitation, which philosophy also teaches. Tragedy should instruct princes; it therefore requires nobility of action and nobility in its principal character.

I believe that this discussion of a matter which is still unsettled in the minds of many confirms the view which I have previously propounded. We ought not make use of ancient regulation which prevents more suitable present-day rules from aiding playwrights. For all artistic practice reveals that nothing is so absolute and perfect in its original condition that it cannot be improved upon.

CHAPTER XV

OF THE UNITIES OF TIME AND PLACE

Now to discuss briefly those prescriptions concerning the length of time within which dramatic action can transpire and a comedy can satisfactorily be concluded.

Aristotle has forbidden a dramatic action to last longer than a twenty-four hour period.[18] Yet his position was hardly held by the ancient playwrights themselves. (I shall not mention here more modern playwrights.) Father Cygneus of our Order in his *Poetics* says with regard to Comedy (Article 10)), that "Hercules in [Plautus'] *Amphitryon* was not able to be conceived and born within the same day, or rather more precisely, within the same night, no matter what its length; nor in [his] *The Captives* could Philocrates leave Aetolia and return to Aulis in a single day."[19] "Nor," says Scaliger, speaking about Greek tragedy, "could Theseus send a message immediately from Athens to Thebes, even with an army of messengers to announce his victory at the end of the battle."

Of course it is a fact that all of Seneca's tragedies occur exactly in one day. Yet he violates many other artistic prescriptions of the ancients, as Father Juventius points out in his *Ratio discendi et docendi*, Chapter 3. Or, can the number of hours which apparently pass in [Plautus'] *The Rope* really be counted as one day? What about the number of hours which pass in his *The Twin Menaechmi* and in *The Three-Penny Day*? Likewise Terence in his *The Andrian Woman* first has a false marriage and then a real one take place. He also in one day has Crito come in the space of a moment from Andros to Athens, opportunely espy Pamphilus in love with a stranger, disown him and accept him back again as his son.

What about plays of more recent vintage? If we inspect the playbills or the printed editions of tragedies and comedies which have appeared in the past century and a half or so, we will discover just how few have conformed precisely to the old prescriptions. And yet these plays have earned applause and warmly deserved the praise which was accorded them. Of course, loosely structured dramatic materials are considered as examples of fine poetic playwriting, even though they are hardly different from epic poetry in which a somewhat freer form is sanctioned. So also says Balbinus in his *Verisimilia*, Chapter 8, Section 1, Number 3. This law (that of a twenty-four hour time period, or one circuit of the sun) I do not consider especially significant, and if it is violated I do not think it a crime, for I am merely following the example set by the ancient playwrights themselves.

The question of probability now arises. Since everything ought to be represented in a theatre as it occurs in actual life it is a violation of the laws of probability to display on stage within a limited number of hours what ordinarily would take months to accomplish. Why, therefore, do I take such delight in seeing something performed within the space of three or four hours (for actors cannot usually perform well past this limit), which cannot even occur within a twenty-four hour time span? The answer is that choral interludes, episodes and scenes are inserted which help to beguile the mind of the spectator into thinking that a much greater period has passed than the actual three or four hours of performance time. Why then should not the same insertions be utilized to extend the apparent time from twenty-four hours to several days or even months?

In arriving at this conclusion I do not wish to condemn, on the one hand, those who do not strictly adhere to time unity in their plays, nor on the other to grant them absolute freedom. I believe that a playwright can make the action fit nicely and according to all probability within the confines of a single day, even though it actually does or can transpire over a much longer time period. This can be accomplished if we presuppose that most of the time has already elapsed, so that the play begins in the middle or towards the end of the story, when only a single day is needed to complete the action. The example of Plautus' *Amphitryon* may be used to demonstrate this construction. As the play begins Amphitryon has just returned home and his servant Sosia recounts to the audience what has previously occurred. Then the playwright proceeds to dramatize the rest of the story within a day's time. The same situation pertains in Plautus' *The Rope*, where the play begins directly following the tempest, and in his *The Ghost* which commences when the old man arrives.

Of course, it is most artistic to create a great variety of incidents which could in all probability occur within the same time span as that required to perform them on stage. It makes the action more believable and the audience react more strongly. No one denies that dramas which follow this precept are deserving of great praise. But by the same token not every play, no matter how ingenious its construction, should be condemned if its plot fails to resolve everything within twenty-four hours time. For it should be remembered that it is one thing to tell a story as history and another to tell it as poetry—to make a tale accord with historic fact and to make it accord with poetic probability. It does not seem absurd to me if the events of many years are presented on stage. Many writers have done so in their plays. Sometimes spectators account an action probable because it is the strict counterpart of nature. Yet at other times spectators are not beguiled into thinking what has happened at one particular time is what happens regularly, even under the most divergent circumstances. The imitation of nature and verisimilitude take precedence over other Aristotelian playmaking rules for men of discernment.

And now to discuss the unity of place. There are some who are so firmly rooted in their conviction as to believe that the locale should remain unchanged and fixed throughout the entire course of the play, be that spot a garden, harbor, forest, hall or house. Would not the observance of so rigid a law, it seems to me, ban many an outstanding play from performance? Tragedy generally demands that its parts be in strongest contrast, with each section having its own peculiar locale and different action. Consequently there must be different scenes for each. Let us suppose that characters of strikingly contrasting personality were not to be allowed to appear in the same play. We should say that this flies in the face of all experience and good sense. It would follow, then, that changing scenery is permissible. Of course, we frown on those who pass off their work as artistic tragedy when they are merely displays of scenic effects intended solely for superficial entertainment. Such displays present a palace at one moment, a garden at another, then a forest, thereafter an armed camp, a seascape, and so on. I believe that we should be guided by what verisimilitude admits and nature demands. If a change of scene will provide pleasure, then let it be done following the end of an act, or after a choral interlude. These choral interludes themselves afford opportunities for scenic change. But scenes should not always be joined together in the same monotonous fashion; rather they should be arranged to fit the situation within each act so that one character comes upon another. As a result the stage is never completely empty: either a new character appears to overhear a conversation without the speakers being aware of his presence, or another character comes on stage as two characters are exiting, or a second character enters to talk with another character already on stage. In consequence of this convention of scenic liaison, I do not see how scenery can be changed during the course of an act with the actor on stage in front of it. It would be incompatible with the course of nature to have a person at one moment in a hall and the next in a garden, unless the playwright means to suggest the occurrence of some kind of miracle—a magical transportation from one place to another. Consequently scenery changes required by changes of locale should take place at the end of each act or choral interlude, for in this way verisimilitude is preserved.

CHAPTER XVI

ON THEATRICAL DISPLAY

I do not wish to deny that many pleasant displays and spectacles are regularly presented as interludes between the acts because spectators enjoy them. Provided they are used discretely and with moderation they can interest and move an audience. In this matter, therefore, I only counsel moderation and to beware of excess. The playwright should remember that these interludes are means to an end and not the end itself. It is no small error for a playwright to set such great store in display that he must embellish his stage with lavish effects. Then when the audience has been diverted by such curiosities, he thinks he is a veritable Roscius.

Here are a few examples of such displays: Mercury flies through the air. A war is fought between the herons and the vultures. A devil from the infernal regions carries off souls through the clouds, then dives into a smoking pit out of which emerge crackling flames and horrid shapes. A triple-forked lightning bolt thunders out of a cloud and smashes into a tower, destroying the wicked. A duel to the death is fought between swordsmen. A military drill is held wherein a company of soldiers assembles, forms skirmish lines, waves its banners and forms a testudo by holding shields overhead like a roof. Such creations of symbolic figures and others like them can, if arranged pleasingly and used in moderation, prove enjoyable and stir the emotions of the audience.

Court theatres should be allowed more lavish display because they are better endowed with resources and mechanical contrivances than are schools. But because our Jesuit academies lack such influence does not mean that we cannot compete successfully with court theatres. We can supply art in our acting which a machine play cannot match. More than once I have seen great men deeply moved by the performance of a single scene; they were not at all concerned about the meagerness of the scenery or the plainness of the costumes, for artistry in acting compensated for the lack of visual display. Hence the playwright should not despair of gaining success even if his work does not have the fulsomeness of decoration with which a stage may be dressed. A native talent combined with practical handworking skill can produce something from nothing in this area. Just how to teach this art or to note is down for others to follow I frankly do not know. One must obtain this knowledge through natural aptitude and ability. If this propensity is lacking, no instruction can compensate for its absence. Those who have this talent do not need to be taught, for they can create what is appropriate and novel for a scene quite easily by themselves.

But in order to treat the subject of theatrical spectacle for the small stage at some length, let me begin by stating categorically that a playwright above all should take care that the spectacular effects which he has so cleverly contrived are based upon ideas which are germane to the play itself. They should not be far-fetched notions which are dragged in, but allegorical illusions to the plot or references in parable form to other aspects of the drama. I am led to this conclusion by the fact that clever creations of this kind are a delight to men of intelligence who understand the extent to which elegance in pageantry should go—that it is suitable only if it contributes and relates to the meaning of the play and the meaning of the symbolism is clear to the audience. For even within the confines of a small stage, without extensive machinery, such clever creations can be effected. In my opinion, the real basis on which all theatrical display rests is the idea that it should complement the play and make it agreeable to the spectators. If I have not been able to make myself sufficiently clear, perhaps an example or two will better express what I have in mind.

A vain youth, while contemplating his image in a mirror, sees a death's head reflected in the glass. Then the head of Christ, crowned with thorns, appears and gazes at him. He thereupon is converted to a better life. This display will require some art and ingenuity to make the changes which must occur within the mirror.

Another youth sits by a fountain. From its basin a jet of water supports a small ball in the air. After a time the jet allows the ball to descend, then spins the ball up again into the air, then once more allows it to drop into the basin. In this repetition the youth takes stock of the inconstancy of mortality and resolves to place his trust in eternal things.

The corruption of innocent and pious youth may be revealed in the followed manner. A painter paints a charming picture of a youth on a canvas. For a while the portrait remains as beautiful as ever on the artist's easel. Then avarice discernibly grows in its features, and, with an inky hand, defiles the once beautiful face. The spectators are saddened, yet they recognize what depravity can do to those who lack modesty and propriety.

A similar theatrical interlude can be created showing a youth lying on his bed immersed in thoughts of shameful delight. But, states the playwright, he is damning himself forever. For as he is lying there, Cupid appears equipped with a flaming arrow. He stealthily creeps to the couch on which the youth is lying, applies a powdery preparation to the point of the dart and spreads it over the chest of the youth. Kindled by this incendiary power, symbolic of his lustful thoughts, the young man goes up in flames. Soon death appears and drives a fatal spear into the youth's body, thereby dispatching his miserable soul to eternal perdition.

Another spectacle I have seen concerns Prince Casimir whose blessed, loving heart was equipped with wings so that it might fly to the lap of the Virgin Mother untouched by base sensuality.

I have otherwise seen a playwright bring two friends on stage. Then Love appears who takes their two hearts and melts them down in a kettle on a hearth, then pours back into both of them the one infusion—the symbol of true friendship.

I shall not add any more lest I seem to be overflowing with such examples. It suffices if I have given the expert reader some idea as to how he might create his own symbolic displays.

For theatrical displays of this kind some mention of costume should now be made. Good taste in stage dress not gained by sanctioning materials which are cheap and commonplace, shapeless and inelegant, affected or contrary to familiar custom and usage to be introduced on stage. Also the qualities of the character should be apparent through his dress and accessories—what rank he possesses, what his duties are and what he represents. Thus a soldier is recognizable by his spear and sword, a carpenter by his hammer and tools, a farmer by his hoe, a lawyer by his robe, an initiate into a priestly order by the fillet about his head, a musician by his harp and lute, a painter by his brushes and palette, and a sailor by his oars.

The gods of the ancient fables have their own peculiar symbols as well. Jupiter has an eagle and holds a bolt of lightning in his hand. Juno is accompanied by peacocks and Venus carries doves. Flora is girdled with flowers, Ceres with ears of corn, Pomona carries fruit, Neptune bears a trident, Pluto a wand or keys, Mars a round shield and spear, Apollo a lyre, Bacchus ivy, Momus a mask, Cupid a bow and arrows, Hercules a club, the fauns and satyrs carry flutes, and the rivers bear urns.

Descriptions of the insignia of the gods, of the vices and virtues, and of the most diverse kinds of figures and personages may be found in the appendix to this small volume. These may prove of advantage as a general guide to the playwright for costuming the interludes, since they have been catalogued and arranged in alphabetical order. Father Jacob Masenius S.J., has collected a great number of them in his *Speculum imaginum* (Mirror of Appearances). Some also have been taken from other authors. By being able to inspect these symbolic figures the playwright may be inspired to create his own pleasing interludes, depending, of course, upon the theatrical resources at his disposal. Playwrights should find a gold mine of information in these symbolic figures for use during these theatrical exhibitions, providing the material is properly handled. Though the list could be longer, what is here represented is sufficient to allow the dramatist to copy the figures and to use them in his own way. Masenius, from whose book we have borrowed these figures, can provide more of the same for those wishing to become even more familiar with the subject.

FOOTNOTES

1. Lang is referring here specifically to rhetoricians like Amadeus Bajocensis, Nicholas Caussinus and Johannes Voellus who had formulated principles for the preacher and sermonizer.
2. A paraphrase of line 83 of Plautus, *Stichus*, Act I, Sc. 2.
3. *Poetices libri septem* (Lyon, 1561), "Persona est res animata, ficta in Scena, verae imitatrix."
4. Cf. Cicero, *De Oratore* 55, and Jean Voël, *Artficium generale texendae sive componendae orationis,* p. 113.
5. *Cf.* Cicero, *De Oratore*, 55 and (attributed to Cicero), *Rhetorica ad Herennum* III, 19. "Delivery in its entirety consists of two parts, voice and gesture, whereof the first works its effect upon the ear, and the second upon the eye, by which two senses all sensation penetrates the soul," *Institutio oratoria* XI, 3,14.
6. Lang here has paraphrased Cicero, *De Oratore,* III, 217–219.
7. "The art of modulation gives charm to the voice and continuously refreshes the ears. What is called *monotonia* in Greek—that uniform strain of sound and breath—should also be avoided . . . by using the ability of the mind to produce certain slight changes in the voice at various intervals during the speech and at its starting places and transitions as determined by the sense of the words and the nature of the thoughts." Quintilian, *Institutio oratoria* XI, 3, 44–46.
8. Lang here is no doubt referring to Aristotle's *Rhetoric* and *Poetics,* as well as the *Rhetorica ad Alexandrum.*
9. Lang quotes the Latin form accurately, though here omitting the qualifications pertaining to completeness, magnitude, speech and performance. These he later supplies in the last part of this chapter.
10. Jakob Bidermann, *Ludes theatrales sacri sive opera comica posthuma* (Munich 1666), *Praemonitio ad Lectorem,* Sheet (+) 2r – v.
11. *Ibid..* Sheet (+) 5v.

12. *Ibid.*, Sheet (+) 6.
13. *Ibid.*, Sheet (+) 7r.
14. Alessandro Donati, *De Arte Poetica*, Book 2, Chapter 11.
15. LeJay, *Bibliotheca Rhetorum*, Vol. II, p. 17.
16. Jouvency, I, ii, 2. See Gilbert C. Lozier, *A Translation of Jouvency's "Method of Learning and Teaching" with Historical Significance* (Ed.D. Dissertation, University of Cincinnati, 1957), pp. 75, 77.
17. *The Poetics*, Chapter VI.
18. Aristotle, *Poetics*, Chapter V.
19. *De Arte poetica, libri duo* (Liège 1664), Vol. II, p. 256.
20. *Poetices libri septem.*

GLOSSARY OF NAMES

BAJOCENSIS Amédée de Bayeaux, a member of the Capuchin order whose work on homiletic theory, *Paulus eccelsiastes seu Eloquentia christiana qua orator evangelicus ad ideam et doctrinam Divi Pauli formatur* (1662) was widely read and used by other orders as well.

BALBINUS Bohuslav Balbin S.J., (1621–1688), a Bohemian historian and linguist, author of *Verisimilia humaniorum disciplinarum, seu judicium privatum de omni litterarum* n.p., n.d. a comprehensive review of principles pertaining to all communicatory arts including rhetoric and poetry.

JAKOB BIDERMANN S.J. (1578–1639), probably the most formidable playwriting talent produced by the Society of Jesus. *Cenodoxus, Der Doktor von Pariss,* [sic], was his masterpiece. Orginally written and performed in Latin it was later translated into German. The play concerns a Faust-like necromancer who sells his soul for knowledge and reputation, and is finally condemned to perdition. Bidermann drew his material from a legend about St. Bruno of Cologne who was so moved by the horrifying end of this famous, outwardly pious teacher at the University of Paris, that he founded the Cartesian Order in 1086. So powerful was the impact of Bidermann's play in its 1609 performance, that, according to contemporary report, no less than fourteen prominent members of the nobility, as well as private citizenry including the actor playing the leading role entered the Society of Jesus. The German version of the play may be found in Willi Flemming's *Barockdrama* (Vol. II, *Das Ordensdrama)* Hildesheim, 1965, pp. 47–183.

CASIMIR, Prince of Poland (1460–1483) and son of King Casimir IV, who wished him to seize the throne of Hungary. When the son refused to use violence to achieve this objective, his father caused him to be imprisoned for three months. The prince spent the remainder of his life in a state of self-imposed prayer, study and celibacy. He is today the patron saint of Poland and Catholic Lithuania.

CAUSSINIUS, Nicholas Caussin S.J., confessor to Louis XIII, playwright and author of *Tragoediae sacrae* (1620) and the rhetorical work *De Eloquentia sacra et humana* (Louvain 1617).

DONATUS, also known as Alessandro Donati S.J., (1584–1640). He wrote an *Ars poetica* in 1631 in which he contended that saints and martyrs were fitting subjects for dramatic presentation, thus broadening the compass for the central figure of tragedy and thereby diverging from the narrow neoclassic formulary.

MARTIN DUCYGNE (Cygneus) S.J., (1619–1669), professor of rhetoric and a widely acclaimed rhetorician. He was the author of *Ars Metrica sive ars condendorum eligantiorum versuum* (Liège 1664) and other works on poetic composition.

ST. JOHN [Calabytes] (c. 450), who lived as a hermit. He disguised his identity from his parents while partaking of their charity. The subject of a play by Bidermann.

ST. JOSEPHAT, Bishop of Catholic Lithuania who was martyred by a schismatic in 1623 and the subject of a play by the Jesuit playwright, Jakob Bidermann.

JUVENTUS, Joseph Jouvency (1643–1719), edited among other works the *Ars poetica* of Horace. He is most famous for his *Christianis litterarum magistris de ratione discendi et docendi* published in Paris in 1685 and in later editions. Lang obtained his material on delivery from the Second Part, Chapter 9, entitled *Ratio pronunciandi*, of the work, intended for the instruction of teachers in the Jesuitical academies. Jouvency was also the author of ten school dramas and was thus familiar with the application of rhetorical method to the stage.

GABRIEL FRANÇOIS LEJAY S.J. (1657–1734), French contemporary of Franz Lang and author of *Bibliotheca Rhetorum praecepta et exempla complectens, quae tam ad oratoriam facultatem quam ad poeticam pertinent. Discipulis pariter Magistris perutilis* (Paris 1725), a collection of rules and illustrations for oratory and theatrical performance. Of special interest is *Liber de choreis dramaticis*, pp. 521–528, of the *Bibliotheca*, which is devoted to an exhibition of the art of the dance. Father LeJay was also distinguished as a playwright and as the teacher of Voltaire.

MASENIUS, Jakob Masen (1606–1681), Jesuit schoolman and dramatist. He is the author of *Speculum imaginum veritatis occultae, exhibens symbola, emblemata, hieroglyphica, aenigmata, omni tam materiae quam formae varietate, exemplis simul, ac praeceptis illustratum* (Cologne 1650), an 1120 page compendium of verbal and pictorial allegorical representations used in Jesuit theatrical productions during the seventeenth century. Masen is also well known for his dramatic theories propounded in *Palaestra eloquentiae ligatae dramatica* (1654–1657), excerpts of which may be found in Willi Flemming's *Barockdrama*, Vol. II, *Das Ordensdrama* (Hildesheim 1965), pp. 37–46.

SYLVESTER MAURUS, S.J., (1619–1687). Scholiast and author of a commentary on Aristotle, *Aristotelis opera quae extant omnia brevi paraphrasi ac litterae perpetuo inhaerente explanatione illustrata,* in six volumes published in Rome in 1668.

JACOB PONTANUS (Spanmüller) S.J., of Brux, Bohemia (1542–1626), was the author, inter alia, of *Progymnastica latinatis sive dialogi* in three volumes published at Augsburg, Bavaria between 1588 and 1594 and reprinted in various editions to the eighteenth century. The work was in use in Protestant as well as in Catholic schools. It contained model Latin compositions written in a warm but classic style. Such subjects as the school, the home, patriotism and national culture, science, art, history and geography were used as the bases for the students' own writing and speaking. It also contained a number of school dramas to be performed by the students as exercises (*progymnasmata*). Pontanus also wrote an early treatise on poetics (*Poeticarum institutionum libri tres,* Ingolstadt, 1594). He was famous as well for having been the teacher of the renowned Jesuit dramatist, Jakob Bidermann.

SOARIUS Cyprien Soarez, S.J. (1524–1593), Spanish-Portuguese humanist and rhetorician, author of *De Arte rhetorica libri tres ex Aristotele, Cicerone et Quinctiliano deprompti,* first published at Coimbre, c. 1560, and reprinted several times thereafter.

VOELLUS, Jean Voël S.J., the French rhetorician and author of *Artficium generale texendae sive componendae orationis* (Dôle 1589), and *De Oratore libri iv ex Cicerone potissimum collecti* (Lyon 1610).

Figure I. By permission of the British Library.

Figure II. By permission of the British Library.

Figure III. By permission of the British Library.

Figure IV. By permission of the British Library.

Figure V. By permission of the British Library.

Figure VI. By permission of the British Library.

Figure VII. By permission of the British Library.

Figure VIII. By permission of the British Library.

SYMBOLIC IMAGES ESPECIALLY USEFUL IN THEATRICAL PERFORMANCE AND COSTUMING

A

Abstinentia a malo (Abstinence from Evil)

A figure wearing a crown who sits by a pillar and gazes upon Tablets of the Law before her. Under her feet are serpents and tortoises which represent sinners, especially those who are filled with lust. Broken arrows are also present in the scene, as well as a kneeling camel. Its ability to abstain from drink is suggestive of continence.

Abundantia (Abundance)

A figure wearing a magnificent dress, a garment woven of green and gold materials. She carries in her hand either a bundle of corn or a horn-of-plenty, or else a bag full of fruit.

Acedia (Fretfulness)

A figure carrying an unstrung bow or a lyre with its string loose, or even cooling herself with a fan.

Adolescentia (Adolescence)

A figure in a varicolored garment, crowned with flowers. She displays in her hand a vase of flowers.

In all entries, the sex of the figure derives from the Latin grammatical gender of the word in question. We may surmise that other figures mentioned in the *Symbolicae imagines* section of the *Dissertatio* have specific reference to particular allegorical representations found in the Jesuit drama of the seventeenth century with which Lang was familiar.

Adulatio (Flattery)
A figure plays a flute. At her feet is a deer and a hive from which bees are flying.

Aër (Air)
A figure sitting on a cloud, while comets freely pass by. She has a peacock near her and is surrounded by many birds. Or she may have a chameleon instead.

Aestas (Summer)
A figure in a yellow dress, wearing a crown of spikes of grain. In her right hand she has a burning torch, or she may carry in a similar fashion a sickle for reaping.

Aeternitas (Eternity)
A figure dressed in cerulean blue with distinctive golden stars, who carries a globe or a serpent in the shape of a circle.

Agricultura (Agriculture)
A figure dressed in a rustic habit, with a green tunic and an ornate crown of spikes of grain. She holds in her hand a shrub bearing early flowers or a hoe with which she cultivates the soil.

Alchymia (Alchemy)
An old philosopher among his alembics, flasks, beakers and glasses, and bellows and other instruments for making a charcoal fire burn more brightly in a furnace. He studies in amazement one of his vessels which has just broken.

Ambitio (Ambition)
A female figure with her clothes closely wrapped about her, and eyes veiled, who has many crowns in her hands. She considers what occupation—civil, military or naval—will bring her honors.

Amicitia (Friendship)
A figure dressed in white, crowned with myrtle and purple-colored fruit.

Amicitia fucata (False Friendship) Two figures with their left hands embracing each other with a mask in their respective hands. A fox is lying near their feet.

Amnestia (Amnesty)

An armed warrior who offers, nevertheless, an olive branch as a sign of peace.

Amor (Love)

Amor Divinus (Divine Love). A winged figure, on whose head is a crown on top of which there may be a sun, who carries a bow and golden arrow in his hand. Or similarly the head of Phoebus, crowned with the sun's rays in whose hand there is a torch. Or whose head is encircled with flames and who carries in his hand a heart emitting fire. Or a figure whose shoulders sprout wings and on whose breast is written the name JESUS. In his hand there is a flaming heart pierced by a spear.

Amor (Love) or *Cupido* (Desire) sometimes is shown as a figure with a bow and arrows, and sometimes as a blindfolded figure carrying torches or snares.

Amor Patria (Patriotism). A victorious warrior wearing a wreath of sweet grass or else of oak leaves.

Amor Suiipsius (Self-Love). A figure carrying a mirror in which he sees himself reflected, or holding an ape in his hand or a shield. Also *Philautia*, the name of an allegorical character in the *Cenodoxus* of Bidermann (q.v. *supra*, Chapter XIV, p. 80).

Amor conjugalis (Conjugal Love). Two hearts tied to each other with the same cords.

Amor Mundi (Worldly Love). A blindfolded youth leaning on a globe and holding a broken reed in his hand. At his feet lies a small vessel filled with all kinds of flowers. Other flowers are strewn roundabout, from which snakes are emerging.

Aprilis (April)

The delightful form of a winged boy, crowned with myrtle and handsomely dressed in green. He displays in his right hand the zodiacal Taurus the Bull, which sign is surrounded by flowers. In his left hand he holds a basket bursting with fruit.

74 PERFORMING ARTS RESOURCES

Aqua (Water)

A figure sitting on a cloud bearing in her right hand a scepter and in her left a pitcher from which water is pouring. All about water reeds and canes are growing.

Architectura (Architecture)

A figure with various types of architectural instruments, as well as the ground plan of a building.

Aristocratia (Aristocracy)

A figure dressed in costly garments sitting on a throne. His right hand carries a fasces and his left a helmet. Heaps of gold and silver coins are at his feet.

Arithmetica (Arithmetic)

A figure who sits near a numerical table, at the head of which are the signs *par* (equal to) and *impar* (unequal to). Or else the figure writes *par, impar* on a white tablet with an iron stylus.

Astraea (Goddess of Justice)

A winged figure who holds a rod in her hand. See *Justitia* (Justice).

Astrologia (Astrology)

A figure wearing a crown of stars dressed in clothing embroidered in constellations. On her breast is a sun. In her right hand is a scepter, while she holds a globe in her left. She may also have an eagle painted on her shield.

Audacia (Audacity)

A man in complete armor with a sword and a shield on which is inscribed *per tela, per enses* (by spear and sword).

Aulicus (A Courtier)

A youth standing in the shade of a tree to which ivy clings. He holds a barometer in which the liquid is rising and falling, while he leans upon a globe at his feet. At his side there is a bagpipe, deflated, flat and silent.

Aurora (Dawn), or *Oriens Sol* (Sunrise)

A winged figure in a remarkable yellow dress who carries a torch in her hand. In addition flowers may be present which Aurora produces and causes to grow. Or, she may have a glittering star on her head and be dressed in a red tunic ornamented with pearls.

Authoritas (Authority)

Holds a scepter and matching keys, denoting strength of command. Or the figure holds a scale and weapons.

Autumnus (Autumn)

A figure dressed like a vintner, with a crown of vine leaves and carrying a bunch of grapes and a cornucopia.

Avaritia (Avarice)

A pale, emaciated melancholy figure carrying a closed sack and a shield, on the front of which is a greedy-looking wolf and the inscription, ΠΛ/ΥΤΟΣ (Plutus, the God of Wealth).

B

Bellona (Roman Goddess of War)

A figure whose hair is falling loose from beneath a blood-red helmet. She carries a whip in her right hand and, in her left, a round shield on which is a wolf. Or, like the Goddess Athena, she carries a spear in her right hand and a shield of Medusa in her left.

Benignitas (Kindness)

Wears a golden crown on which is displayed a prominent sun-disk. In one hand she has a spray of pine needles, and in the other a shield on which is an elephant.

Berecynthia or *Cybele* or *Terra* (Earth)

A nature goddess of Phrygia and Asia Minor, variously called Berecynthia, Cybele, or The Great Idaean Mother. On her head she wears a towering crown and in her hand she carries a key, because in winter she locks her wealth away in the earth and in the spring she brings it out again. She rides in a triumphal car drawn by lions. She wears a dress decorated with flowers and figures of various animals.

Bonitas (Benevolence)

Has on her shield a pelican which nurtures its young with blood flowing from its own heart.

Boreas (The North Wind)

A figure which has the tail and feet of a dragon, but without its flapping wings. Or, a bristly old man armed with a bellows or a fan for blowing air, with a crown of blackthorn twigs.

C

Calliope (Muse of Epic Poetry)

She wears a crown on her head and carries laurel leaves in her left hand and in her right hand books—*The Iliad* of Homer, *The Odyssey*, *The Aeneid*, etc.

Castitas (Chastity)

A maid dressed as a vestal in white, symbolic of desire subdued. Or a maiden in white with her head veiled who carries a scepter in one hand and turtle doves in the other. Or a woman dressed like Pallas Athena with an engraved helmet who carries a defeated cupid. A purple flower (they call it *amelinus* in Italy) is evident on her shield.

Chorographia, Descriptio Regionum
(Description of Regions of the Earth)

A figure wearing a garment made of double-colored bombazine twill, who measures the diameter and circumference of a terrestrial globe.

Clementia (Clemency)

A figure extending an olive branch about whose feet are heaps of armor, or else scattered arms may be painted on shields.

Comoedia (Comedy)

Carries a flute in her left hand and a mask in the other. Or she may hold a scroll on which may be read: *Describo mores hominum* (I imitate the customs of men).

Concilium (Advice)

An old man clad in a scarlet robe with a chain about his neck on which a kind of heart is pendent. He holds a book in his right hand and a night-raven or an owl in his left.

Concordia (Concord)

Carries a small bundle of darts on which a pair of doves may be sitting. She has a crown of olive leaves on her head. Or Concord may be represented by a maiden dressed in ancient fashion with a wreath of flowers who carries in her right hand a libation bowl in which there is a human heart. In her left hand are sticks bound tightly into a bundle. Or by a woman who carries the lyre of Apollo under her right arm and a pair of united hearts in her left hand. To designate military concord, Athena may be shown holding a spear in her right hand and a serpent in her left.

Concupiscentia (Sexual Desire)

A quiet, smiling crocodile suddenly seizes a partridge with whom it has been playing.

Conscientia (Conscience)

A figure whose upper garments are white, and whose lower are black, carries a file in her right hand. On her breast a heart stung by a snake is visible.

Conscientia bona (Good Conscience) sits in a bed of roses under a Cross, and holds a lamp and carries a book on a page of which a heart is depicted. The heart, which is upright, is encircled by a snake, the symbol of eternity.

Conscientia mala (Bad Conscience) is a maddened figure having an injured heart in one hand while the other grasps a torch. As with Medusa, serpents are nestling on her head. At her feet may be seen short swords, a rope, a glass full of poison, an open pit and a snarling dog.

Conscientia remorsus (Remorseful Conscience). A figure wearing a white outer garment and an inner one of black, who holds the moon in his right hand and in his left a heart bitten by a serpent.

Consortium malorum (Consorting with Evil Persons) or *Societas mala* (Bad Company)

A figure holds a forked pole (for spreading bird-nets), which is smeared with bird-lime, in his right hand; a snake coils about his left arm. At his feet a cat (the symbol of an evil, perfidious consort) rubs against him. But while it licks him, it frequently and unexpectedly scratches him with its claws.

Constantia (Constancy)

A figure wearing a military habit and cloak, with helmet on her head, carries a scepter in her left hand. Or, she may use her left hand to embrace a column, and may hold a sword in her right. She may also display a shield with the device of a hand and a sword and glowing coals.

Contritio (Contrition) or
Poenitentia (Penitence)

A figure crowned with hyssop, a plant whose twigs were used in Biblical rites of purification. He is holding in one hand a sprig of olive and in the other a rod or whip and a piece of paper containing these words: *Delictum meum cognitum tibi feci* ("I have made known to you my own offence," Psalm 31:5) In this [stage] picture he beats his breast with his fist and looks imploringly heavenward while extending his left hand upward.

Cosmographia (Cosmography)

A figure dressed in cerulean blue embroidered with stars. On one side she has a celestial, and on the other a terrestrial, globe. Moreover she holds other mathematical instruments, including an astrolabe, in her hands.

Crudelitas (Cruelty)

An armed figure with a helmet in the shape of a tiger, who carries a sword in her right hand and holds up a gory human head in her left.

Curiositas (Curiosity)

Has a dress embroidered with pictures of human ears and of frogs. On her back are wings.

D

Democratia (Democracy)

Wearing a crown covered with vine leaves, she has a dark-red apple in her right hand and serpents in her left. To one side there is a sack brimming with grain.

Desiderium (Longing)

A figure which may have a flame in its heart which the left hand shelters, while the right hand extends heavenward. On a shield is a symbol of a deer drinking water from a spring.

Desiderium generosum (Noble Longing). A youthful warrior wrestles down a lion and rips its tongue from the beast's throat.

Desperatio (Despair)

A figure whose one hand stabs at her breast, while the other holds a branch of cypress.

Detractio (Withdrawal)

A figure dressed in a torn garment carrying a trumpet in one hand and a sword in the other.

Devotio (Devotion)

With one hand a figure kindles a flame on a sacrificial altar and with the other she touches her breast. Or she may hold a candle in her hand. See *Pietas* (Pity) and *Religio* (Religion).

Diligentia (Diligence)

Holds a water clock or a shield on which is depicted a stone wound about with ivy, or a spur in one hand and a clock in the other. Or, she may carry a bunch of thyme in one hand around which bees are swarming, while the other holds a bundle of almond and mulberry twigs.

Discordia (Discord)

Has a head of hair like snakes and holds a burning torch in her right hand and a sack filled with lawsuits in her left. Or she may carry a lighted torch and a swollen moneybag. Or else she may be dressed in particolor and carry a device for making fire with flint. Or just as the garments of the Furies of Hell are made up of all sorts of flaming colors, so she is also dressed in blood-red clothing, etc.

Discretio (Discretion)

Holds a sieve in her right hand and a rake in her left.

Divinitas (Divinity)

A figure dressed in white whose head is surrounded by flames. She has in each hand a globe of different colors from which fire is emerging.

Doctrina (Instruction)

Holds in her left hand a scepter on the top of which is an image of the sun. An open book rests on her lap, while heavenly dew clings to her head.

Dolor (Grief)

A melancholy, pale man, most dismally dressed. He holds a torch which has just been extinguished and is still smoking in his hand. Or his feet may be in chains and he may be stung in the breast by a snake. Or else, he may carry a smoking torch and a branch of absinthe. For *Dolor de peccatis* (Grief from Sin), see *Contritio* (Contrition).

Dolus (Deceit)

Holds a burning bundle of straw. He is disguised in dress and speech.

Dominium (Possession)

Is represented by a king bearing a scepter on the end of which is an eye. He carries a shield on which is painted a man sitting on a lion and goading him with his right hand while holding the lion's reins with his left.

Dubitatio (Doubt)

A figure wandering in the darkness who holds a walking stick in one hand and a lantern in the other.

E

Ecclesia (Church)

A figure holds in her arms a cross intertwined with lilies and roses. In her hands she has a jeweled papal crown and the Mosaic laws. Or in her right hand she may carry a cross and two pendant keys, while a dove perches on top of her tiara.

Eleemosyna (Charity)

A veiled figure carries a lighted lamp in her hand while she distributes alms to the needy.

Elegia (Elegy)

A figure crowned with laurel, dressed in black, who carries a harp.

Eloquentia (Eloquence)

A woman dressed in violet with a spear in her right hand and a lightning bolt in her left. Or she may wear a golden cross as a sign upon her helmet, and hold the lightning in her right hand while offering an open book with her left. Or she can have her shield decorated with a picture of Amphion (the husband of Niobe who helped construct the walls of Thebes by charming the stones into place with his lyre), enchanting the rocks by his singing. Or Eloquence may be represented by an armed hero on whose helmet there is a gold crown and who has a sword strapped to his side and a lightning bolt on his arm which is bare to the elbow. In the other hand is an open book, in which a water clock is depicted.

Endymion

A youth beloved of Luna, whose youth and beauty were preserved by an eternal sleep into which he was cast by the moon goddess. He wears a dark blue garment embroidered with stars and carries a sphere in his right hand.

Erato (Muse of Lyric, Amatory Poetry)

A figure with myrtle and roses falling about her head. She carries a lute in her right hand and a quill in her left. She has a picture of Cupid on her shield.

Europa

A sister of Cadmus, abducted by Zeus, who took the form of a bull, from her home in Europe to Asia Minor. Hence, by extension, Europe. A figure riding on a bull. Or a woman sitting on a double cornucopia: the right one displays a picture of a temple, the left spews scepters, crowns, armor, horses and cattle out upon the earth.

Euterpe (Muse of Music and Lyric Poetry)

A maid crowned with flowers, piping on a reed. At her feet are various kinds of musical instruments.

Exercitatio (Cultivation)

A young man dressed in particolored attire with a water clock on his head and carrying a golden circle in his right hand. Over his left arm is a sheet of paper displaying the word *Encyclopaedia* (A well-rounded education). He has winged feet.

Exilium (Exile)

A man in the dress of a pilgrim, carrying a staff. He holds a peregrine falcon in his left hand.

Experientia (Experience)

A figure having a dress made of cloth-of-gold who holds in her right hand a quadrant and in her left a ten-foot measuring rod from which is suspended the inscription, *Rerum Magistra* (The Instructress in all Matters).

Explorator (A Spy)

A man wrapped in a cloak richly decorated with pictures of eyes and ears. He carries a lantern whose light is concealed. A dog runs before him.

F

Fama (Reputation)

Fama bona (Good Name). Carries a trumpet in her right hand and an olive branch in her left. Or she may have wings and wear a garment replete with pictures of eyes, ears and mouths and be blowing two horns, one high- and the other low-pitched. She can even carry a dark blue banner on which appears the crest or the name of the person she is celebrating.

Fama mala (Bad Name) is represented by a figure with the wings of a bat.

Fames (Famine)

A figure wasted by deprivation, chewing clumps of grass and gnawing on stone.

Fastus (Haughtiness)

Carries a peacock in his hand and has a representation of the globe under his feet. See *Superbia* (Pride).

Fatum (Fate)

Is in the form of a man dressed in a white garment hanging down to his feet. A celestial sphere is in one hand and above it he holds a star. There is a golden chain hanging from the sphere to the ground.

Favor (Favor)

A figure with vine and elm leaves encircling his forehead who holds a puppy or a kingfisher in his lap. Or else he may be a winged youth with blindfolded eyes who displays on his shield the shift from friendship to adulation to malice. [The kingfisher (*halcyon*) was associated with the mythical bird of Greek legend which built its nest in the seas and had the power to charm wind and wave into a state of absolute calm].

Fidelitas (Faithfulness)

A figure dressed entirely in white with one hand holding a seal, the other a key. The seal depicts the following: a beautiful woman is standing upon a stone trampling underfoot a pile of masks, while she displays a mirror in her hand. This means that the friendly mirror reflects what is in front of it; which is to say, that the genius of a friend is to make his features assume the same expression as his fellow's be it sadness or joy, and bravely to face danger for the sake of a friend.

Fides (Faith)

Christiana Fides (The Christian Faith). A figure in white embracing a cross with her right hand and holding an open book. Or else she may carry a sacred chalice, the Law of Moses or the sacred Gospels. On a shield is the motto: *Super hanc petram* ("On this rock" [According to the instructions given by Jesus to Peter, Matthew 16:18.]) For *Fides humana* (Faith in Humanity) or *Fides amicorum* (Faith in friends), see *Fidelitas* (Faithfulness) above.

Felicitas (Happiness)

Felicitas temporalis (Transitory Happiness) can be shown by a figure wearing a magnificent costume on whose head is a moon in the fashion of Diana, sitting at a table with every kind of food and drink most lavishly supplied. Nearby can be seen a chest filled with moneybags. The figure holds a fading rose in her right hand.

Felicitas Mundana (Worldly Happiness) is a female figure expensively dressed in contemporary fashion with a gold-ornamented crown entwined with rotting plants. She carries a scepter in one hand and a libation bowl filled with gems and gold coins in the other.

Felicitas in Communi (Public Happiness) is represented by a figure who holds in her right hand a caduceus, and in her left a horn-of-plenty which symbolize heavenly and earthly goodness, respectively. She can also carry an olive twig or a branch of laurel, which is the symbol of happiness deriving from peace or victory.

Fiducia (Trust)

Has a ship as its symbol. When representing trust in God, a head is shown gazing at a glowing sun. In one hand the figure holds a cross, the other rests on an altar on which a bound book of sacred literature is lying together with a branch containing dark red apples. She is standing upon a bundle of reeds.

Fiducia in mundum (Trust in the World). A figure wearing a crown of reeds holds a sack of money near her. On a table are a scepter, a helmet, a robe and a mirror. Her feet touch on a winged globe while her hand offers a leaf from which apples of Sodom are suspended. One such piece of fruit has burst open and is scattering ashes which are within. To one side a butterfly is fluttering away pursued by a swallow. This means that the sweetest pleasures of the world are cut down by the intervention of death. Trust likewise bears a scepter at whose tip are two clasped hands.

Foecunditas (Fecundity)

A figure, wearing a garland woven of hemp, has in her lap a nest of gold-finches. About her feet there are nesting places and young birds. Or she may hold a cornucopia in her left hand and a little child in her right. Or the cornucopia may be filled with double spikes of grain right up to its small end, as well as other treats popular with mothers of offspring.

Foeneratio (Usury)

An emaciated, twisted, sharp-eyed ancient, wearing armor, who sits among his boxes, bags and various containers for money and shaves coins. Near him there is a table full of scrolls and sealed legal documents. At his rear the Goddess of Misfortune scatters the scrolls with a bellows and makes them fly away. A crow sits on the head of the goddess and flaps its wings. Under her arm is a broken and empty horn-of-plenty.

Fortitudo (Fortitude)

Christianorum fortitudo (Christian Fortitude) or *Virtus Christiana* (Christian Virtue). A figure armed with bright weapons, a helmet on her head decorated with the image of the Holy Ghost, holds with one hand a shield on which is lettered the sign of the cross, while with the other she embraces a cross entwined with laurel leaves. Or she may be crowned with a garland of oak leaves and hold a key in one mouth. Her helmet may be made in the form of a gaping leonine mouth.

Fortuna (Fortune)

Fortuna secunda (Favoring Fortune) leans with her right hand upon a wheel and displays a cornucopia with her left. Or else a wind may blow her hair about her forehead as she sits on a globe, as a crescent-shaped sail fills with wind. Or she may hold a ship's tiller in her right hand.

Fragilitas (Frailty)

A delicate figure whose kerchief is flying away while she holds a bunch of flowers in one hand and a glass dangling from a thread in the other.

Fraus (Fraud)

Is represented as a woman with one neck and two heads, the one young and the other old. In her right hand she has two hearts, in her left a mask. Instead of feet she has the talons of an eagle, and also has the tail of a scorpion. Or she may be a woman in armor with a shield in one hand, while the other holds a bird or fishnet. Or else she may be proffering a handful of flowers from which an adder is uncoiling. See also *Dolus* (Deceit).

Fur (Thievery)

A youth with his head covered by an animal skin. In one hand he carries a dark lantern, in the other a rope-ladder. A knife lies at his feet.

Furia (Fury)

An aged crone dressed in black with a head of horrible black hair. She extends her right arm which holds a whip. In her left is a torch.

Furor (Madness)

A figure of a horrible aspect, spattered with blood, sitting on armor, swords and helmets. She madly roars at her captives whose hands are chained behind their backs. Or Madness may be depicted as a threatening figure of a man in armor carrying a sword in his right hand and in his left a shield on which a lion is painted.

G

Gallia (France)

A figure in military dress carries a spear or a scepter in her left hand. A short striped cloak and chains of gold, heavy Gallic javelins and oblong shields are characteristic. Her sign is the lily.

Garrulitas (Garrulity)

In one hand a figure displays a grasshopper. At her feet a youngster is blowing a bagpipe.

Gaudium (Joy)

Is a female dressed in green and crowned with flowers who carries a Bacchic staff, a pole wound with ivy and vine leaves.

Generositas (Generosity)

A figure dressed in a golden garment, her left hand resting upon the head of a lion, her right hand holding golden chains and other precious gifts which she is presenting to others.

Geographia (Geography)

A figure who has a terrestrial globe at her feet or before her. In her left hand she holds a pair of compasses, in her right a geometric quadrant, as it is known, or else a triangle.

Gloria (Glory)

A figure with a crown of gold holding palm leaves in her right hand and in her left a golden sphere with the signs of the Zodiac. Or Glory may be depicted as a helmeted youth carrying a spear in his left hand and a scepter in his right with his right foot on top of a helmet. Or it may be a winged figure crowned with a royal diadem and carrying a bugle in her right hand and in the other a horn of the goat of Amalthea, a nymph who brought up the infant Zeus on the milk of a goat, or the goat itself. Various crowns of victory can also be added as decoration.

Grammatica (Grammar)

A figure grasping in her left hand a sheaf of papers on which has been written instruction on proper speech and delivery. With her right she waters a plant from a pot she is holding. Or else in her right hand she may point with a ferrule to a slate on which has been written α & ω (Alpha and Omega, the emblem for omniscience). In her left hand she carries a parrot.

Gratia (Grace)

Gratia or *Favor* (Favor). A winged youth, blindfolded, who mounts a chariot. See *Favor* above.

Gratia Divina (Divine Grace). A figure whose head is crowned with loose-streaming bright yellow hair from which light is emanating. With both hands she embraces a cornucopia from which various sorts of good things are flowing. Or a figure with a crown of gold and precious stones who clasps a book and an olive branch in her right hand and a round golden shield in her left.

Gratitudo (Gratitude)

With her right hand she grasps a bunch of bean flowers and with her left a stork. Behind her is an elephant. Or she may hold in one hand a handful of lupine, in the other a nightingale.

Gula (Gluttony)

A figure with a rotund belly and an excessively fat neck who holds a glass in one hand and meat pies in the other.

H

Haeresis (Heresy)

The figure representing heresy has two flames emanating from her mouth. Her hair is tangled. She holds a book in one hand from which a serpent is gliding, and in the other she grasps more serpents. Or it may be represented by a youth armed with a musket from which a book is suspended. He wears a garment sewn from many different colors.

Harmonia (Harmony)

A figure whose head is encircled by a crown, who holds a lute or lyre and a plectrum.

Heroica Virtus (Heroic Virtue)

Hercules with the skin of a lion on his back, a club in his right hand and carrying golden apples in his left.

Historia (History)

Is represented by an angel who writes something in a book while turning away his face. He is placed behind Saturn. Or it may be an angel with his feet securely set on a block of stone. Or else a figure wearing a purple and green garment and carrying a tablet on which has been chiseled the Ciceronian expression: *Testis temporum, lux veritatis, vita memoriae, magistra vitae, nuntia vetustatis* ("The spectator of the seasons, the light of truth, the life of memory, the teacher of life, the messenger of antiquity," Cicero *De Oratore*,II,9,36). Or in her right hand she may hold a reed pen and in her left a book which she places on a writing desk and then proceeds to write.

Honestas (Propriety)

A female figure dressed appropriately and modestly. She conceals her face with a handkerchief.

Honor (Honor)

A victorious hero, his head crowned by palm leaves, a golden chain about his neck, who has metal bands on his arms and carries a lance and a shield on which the picture of two temples are visible. Also apparent are the words *Hic terminus haeret* ("Here a limit is set"). Or, it may be depicted by a figure dressed in the broad-striped toga of peace with the staff and insignia of senatorial rank. Or else a youth with laurel leaves whose neck is ornamented with a golden chain and with bracelets on his arms who is conveyed in a chariot by elephants. Above and at his rear is a diamond in which is set the word *Gloria* (Glory). There may also be a cornucopia.

Honor mundi (Worldly Honor). A figure wearing a crown on his head holds a scepter in his hand. At his feet an open tomb may be seen on which a stone urn is set, filled with drooping and dying flowers.

Horographia (Timekeeping)

Above the head of a winged figure is a water clock. In her left hand is a rule with a pair of compasses, and in her right a sun dial.

Horticultura (Horticulture) or Studium Hortense (The Science of Gardening)

May thus be depicted: Flora, goddess of flowers, crowned with garlands, raises a wreath of blossoms, while Pomona, goddess of fruit carrying a sickle and a horn-of-plenty in her lap, clasps her hand. Directly before them a man covered with the skin of a lion, like Hercules (for it is no light labor to cultivate plants), kneels, sets down a flower basket and plants seeds at the foot of a tree planted in a pot.

Hostilitas (Hostility)

A figure with disheveled hair holds a handful of nettles in her right hand and, in her left a basilisk [a mythological serpent or dragon, able to kill by its poisonous breath].

Humanitas (Humanity)
or *Comitas* (Kindness)

A figure wearing flowers on her dress and carrying a golden chain in her hand. Or else she bears a shield which depicts an elephant on which an Ethiopian is sitting while fondling a dog. This illustrates that all of these animals are friends of man.

Humilitas (Humility)

Is depicted by a figure dressed in white sackcloth with eyes fixed on the ground. In her arms there is a little lamb. She carries a sack of earth and a wicker basket full of bread in her right hand. Or a dove with wings extended may sit on her head. In her right hand she also carries a clove tree which bends towards the earth by reason of the natural force of gravity. A crown and a container filled with precious materials are placed under her feet.

Hydraulica Ars (Hydraulics)

A figure leans on the edge of the fountain and holds a pipe and a pair of compasses in her hand. Two boys alternately pump water through the horns of the Triton statues in the fountain.

Hyems (Winter)

An old woman in a garment of furs sits near a fireplace and indulges in drinking and eating. Or it may be represented by an old man dressed in furs or heavy clothing sitting by a fire, or by a little gnarled old man with a walking stick.

Hymenaeus (Wedding)

A figure crowned with flowers and marjoram wears saffron-colored slippers and has in his left hand a hearth flame (the kind carried by newlyweds), and a torch in his right.

Hypocrisis (Hypocrisy)

A man in a long garment who assumes an expression of piety on his face. He also holds a swan. A lamb and a wolf are at his feet. At one side is a mirror and near it a mask. Just as a mask signifies that things are other than they seem, and a mirror only shows a reflection and not the way things really are, so the swan is the symbol of hypocrisy, for it covers its black skin with the whitest of feathers. Or it may be represented by a woman of blemished appearance sitting on a magnificent tomb (for Christ Himself compared hypocrisy to a whited sepulcher). The woman's hands are joined in devotion (according to the usual manner of praying). Near her is a vase formed in the ancient fashion, on which is a night-owl is perched.

I

Iactantia (Boastfulness)

A boy superbly dressed in precious stones or peacock's feathers who carries a trumpet in his left hand.

Idolatria (Idolatry)

Is depicted as a blind woman offering a bull on an altar. A pagan priest and his attendant also can be present.

Ignorantia (Ignorance)

A blind woman, sumptuously clad, with a crown of poppies who steps barefooted amidst stinging nettles.

Inconstantia (Inconstancy)

A figure with a moon in her hand and a crab underfoot.

Induciae (Truce)

Is designated by a maid bearing a caduceus and holding a round shield in her arms.

Ingratitudo (Ingratitude)

A girl dressed in green ivy holding a serpent in her lap, with flames coming from her mouth and vipers in each hand. Or she may be depicted as a woman holding in her right hand a mirror in which she regards her own image, while with the other she holds a viper. Nearby is set a tree overgrown with ivy. The significance of these objects is that man's good actions are forgotten as easily as the reflection one sees in a mirror. Ingratitude also signifies the reward of evil returned for good. It is specifically conveyed by poisonous vipers emerging from ivy which plant drains the strength of the tree supporting it.

Inimicitia (Enmity)

A figure dressed in black and flame-colored garments who is holding a dragon in her right hand, while in her left she bears a shield on which is seen a dog fighting a cat.

Injuria (Injury)

A figure sticking out his tongue and frothing at the mouth who displays in his right hand a bunch of thorns and stands upon a double-bladed spear.

Injustitia (Injustice)

A figure in a stained white dress who stands with her feet upon a book. One hand holds a toad, the other a sword. Or else Injustice may be depicted as a figure in a bloodstained white garment who has only a single eye on her right side. In her left hand she grasps a golden goblet on which she directs her glance, while with her right she displays a sword. She is dressed in Turkish headgear. Lying on the ground is a balance and the Tables of the Law.

Innocentia (Innocence)

The symbol of innocence is the lamb which is presented either within a heart or on a shield. A palm branch also can be shown. Or else it can be represented as a heart surrounded by thorns from which lilies are budding.

Innocentia servata (Innocence preserved). A winged figure of Time as an elegantly dressed maid with a palm in her hand and carrying a lamb under her arm which she has just snatched from a brutal man, when it sought her aid.

Inobedientia (Disobedience)

A figure whose head is decorated with peacock feathers. Her right hand is raised and she is trampling upon a bridle. An asp presses one of its ears to the ground while closing the other with its tail.

Intellectus (Perception) or Prudentia (Prudence)

A youth dressed in garments of gold with a crown of gold or mustard seed. A flame leaps up from his head. He displays a scepter in his right hand and an eagle in his left. Or else a woman dressed in Trojan costume who holds a sphere in her right hand and a serpent in her left.

Invidia (Envy)

Is conceived as a pale, thin figure with wild eyes, rotting teeth and a venomous tongue, whose spirit is agitated. Or it can be a figure with hair like snakes who consumes her own heart. Or else a little old woman with hard eyes in a costume adorned with dogs, her hair crawling with snakes. Her right hand holds a heart which she may put in her mouth and eat. A snake lies at her left breast. Or envy may be represented by a melancholy woman who tears open that part of her garment which covers her breast. She has bats on her head, in fact, giving the appearance almost of the sun's rays, for envy cannot bear the good fortune of another. A man's skull may also be added to the picture, for we should remember that death was introduced by the devil's envy.

Ira (Anger)

Cupid (representing desire) offers a spear to a man who appears to be attacking with drawn sword. Nearby on a table are seen a bottle, a glass, dice, and playing cards. This shows that anger is often born of impetuosity, drunkenness and gambling. At his feet is a porcupine who, when annoyed, shoots its spines at an attacker. Or else anger may be represented by an armed young woman who has a dragon spitting fire instead of a hound dog. In her right hand she carries a drawn sword, in her left a torch.

J

Judex (A Judge)

An old man dressed in sober garments who carries a remarkable rod wound about with the coils of a serpent in his right hand. On one side is an open book with an eagle. On the other is an hourglass and a stone of Lydia (Lydia was the country of Croesus, hence a precious stone). A naked figure may be glimpsed within a heart suspended from his neck.

Jupiter Planeta (The Planet Jupiter)

A figure crowned with olive. Near him is Sagittarius, the Archer, and an eagle and a thunderbolt.

Jurisdictio (Jurisdiction)

A figure dressed in purple who has the fasces of a consular official.

Jurisprudentia (Jurisprudence)

A matron with an austere face like Lycurgeus, [Spartan lawgiver of the ninth century B.C.] At her rear is a tutelary deity holding a sword and a book. The matron is trampling on a purse which is swollen with coins. Opposite sits a youth surrounded by various books and scrolls who is signing papers which rest upon his knees. Also opposite is a table in the shape of an altar on which lies the fasces of a Roman consul, an imperial crown, a book with a chalice, a priestly fillet and a Bishop's crook. Legal tables are visible at the rear. See also *Jus Canonicum* (Canon Law).

Jus Canonicum (Canon Law)

A matron with a crown of the sun's rays who holds a balance in her right hand. One side of the crown is furnished with a dart and the other with a shining chalice. In her left hand she carries an open book, on which a priestly fillet is evident.

Justitia (Justice)

A queen girt with diadems, carrying a scale in one hand and a sword in the other. About her hand is a necklace on which there is the sign of an eye.

Justitia Rigorosa (Harsh Justice). A skeleton wearing a crown, or death wearing a white shroud. In her right hand she bears a sword, in her left a book.

Juventus (Youth)

A youth in blossom time who carries in his hand a vase of flowers. Under his feet is a crocodile. Also it can be portrayed as the Goddess Hebe, daughter of Juno, who is appointed by Jove as the titular deity of young people.

L

Labor (Toil)

A figure crowned with laurel who wears a cow's hide for clothing and has the wings and feet of a crane as the symbol of indefatigable endurance. At one side is a hoe.

Labor irritus (Toil to no effect).

An Ethiopian washing his body with soap.

Laetitia (Joy)

A figure dressed in a white garment embroidered with leaves and red and yellow flowers. She also wears a crown of blossoms and offers with her right hand a crystalline flagon filled with red wine. In her left hand she extends a golden bowl.

Lascivia (Wantonness)

A figure in a pretentious dress who holds a scorpion in her left hand. At her side is a he-goat and vines. Or it may be a figure sumptuously dressed who holds a mirror in her left hand in which she is inspecting herself while she primps at her hair with her right. Or it may be expressed by a troupe of Satyrs vying with each other in drunkenness.

Lassitudo (Weariness)

A very poorly dressed figure resting on a stick and cooling herself with a fan.

Laus (Praise)

A figure expensively dressed who wears an emerald on her breast and on her figure a crown of roses. She has a horn in her hand which she is blowing.

Lenocinium (Allurement)

An old woman carries, suspended from her girdle, a bag in which letters are wont to be kept. She also has a basket full of flowers, precious materials and fancy gifts.

Lex natura (Natural Law)

A figure sitting in the midst of a garden who carries a hoop in her hand.

Liberalitas (Liberality)

A figure who displays a cornucopia in her left hand and in her right a counting board equipped with beads, which once was the device by which soldiers were paid for their wages. Or it is a figure pouring a pile of coins from a horn-of-plenty. Or the same figure can take a large amount of money from a chest and give it to a boy. Or a figure wearing a golden crown above which a sun is seen who holds in one hand a pine branch. An elephant also can be shown, which is the symbol for kindness.

Libertas (Liberty)

A matron with a liberty cap in her right hand and a cornucopia in her left, as if abundance derives from liberty. Or she may hold a liberty cap in her right hand by which she manumits a bondsman, and a wand by the blow of which, they say, a praetor or consul liberated a slave. Or it may be shown as a youth carrying a broken bridle in his lap who walks up and down on a tight-rope. Or else it may be symbolized by a broken yoke and a liberty cap.

Liberum arbitrium (Free Will)

A young man dressed as a king in garments of various colors, with a crown on his head, holds a scepter in his hand, at the end of which is the letter "Y", which because of its divergence, indicates the possibility of alternate choice.

Lites Forenses (Legal Disputation)

A woman of austere countenance sitting on a judgment seat who has in her lap many petitions, scrolls, codicils or wills from which seals are hanging. She holds a scale in one hand and a laurel wreath in the other. Near her feet an extinguished firebrand is still smoldering. Not far removed is a pair of bellows, for evil advocates are wont to fan the sparks of tiny quarrels into great conflicts. Balloons full of air signify how much court cases are puffed up. And when they are often extended, how they try our patience and are a source of tears.

Logica (Logic)

A young girl with her long hair unbound carries in her right hand a bunch of flowers bound with a ribbon on which is written: *Verum et falsum* (True and false). She holds a serpent in her left hand. Or else she may be veiled, be dressed in white, hold keys in her left hand and extend a sharp spear with her right. Or she may try to untie a knot with her two hands.

Lubentia (Gladness)

A figure with wings on her feet who has a golden apple in her right hand and a handful of flowers in her left, and wears a necklace on her breast.

Luctus (Lamentation)

An adolescent wearing mourning garments.

Ludus (Gaming)
or Alea (Gambling)

A female learning over a table of gaming counters, who puts money into a full purse from which, at the same time, other money is pouring. An anchor, the symbol of hope, is visible at one side. The woman also is touching a wheel of fortune with her foot to check its rotation.

Luna Planeta (The Moon as a Planet)

Should carry a burning torch in her left hand and herbs sacred to Cancer (blight) in her right. Or she may have milky white upper garments while her lower are dark blue. On her head is a moon-disk and in her lap she displays the terrestrial globe.

Lympha (Spring water)

A figure dressed in Venetian costume who may carry a fish on her head and a sprinkling can, that is, a container full of holes used for watering gardens. See also *Aqua* (Water).

M

Magnanimitas (Generosity)

A figure wearing the head of a lion as a helmet and carrying a golden scepter in her hand. Or a figure who stands on a terrestrial globe and holds an eagle which unblinkingly stares at the rays of the sun. Or it may be a matron, dressed in a golden uniform with an imperial crown or diadems on her head, who sits upon a lion. She holds a scepter in her right hand and a cornucopia in her left from which gold is pouring.

Magnificentia (Grandeur)

A figure protected by a helmet in the shape of a lion's head, who scatters money from an Amalthine horn. She holds in her right hand an oval hoop on which are raised marks of lines and arcs, or else she may have a ground plan.

Majestas (Majesty)

A woman with a thunderbolt and a laurel branch. Or she may have a globe and a curule chair, the seat of high officialdom in ancient Rome. The figures of *Gloria* (Glory) and *Acclamatio* (Acclamation) stand at her side. Or she may wear a crown and hold a broken palm branch in her right hand, and lean a bit on some architecture with her left.

Maledicentia (Cursing)

A figure dressed in a dark color, or in green, sticking her tongue out. She holds burning torches in both hands.

Mansuetudo (Gentleness)

A figure crowned with olive leaves who softly cradles a lamb in her arms. Or it may be depicted as a woman decorated with an olive crown who leans with her right hand on an elephant. Or she holds an olive branch in one hand and with the other checks the hand of a boy about to draw a sword. To one side is a little lamb.

Mars

A totally armed figure occupies a chariot driven by a female Fury and drawn by two horses. His right hand shakes a lance, or he may carry a whip.

Mars Planeta (The Planet Mars)

Holds a spear in his left hand while in his right he holds the figure of a cube on a golden base. Nearby is the Scorpion, the eighth sign of the zodiac, associated with aggressive retribution.

Mathesis (Mathematics)

Is represented by a figure dressed in white with wings on her head, a hoop in her right hand and a sundial in her left. On her dress are mathematical symbols.

Matrimonium (Matrimony)

A man defeated and in fetters bowing his neck to the yoke. Or a youth dressed in beautiful clothing carrying a golden ring in his right hand and a yoke on his shoulders. Or a gaily dressed man carrying the marriage yoke on his shoulders who is holding a quince-apple in his hand. His feet are fettered, and beneath them is a watersnake.

Medicina (Medicine)
or Medica Ars (Medical Art)

A figure wreathed with laurel who holds a cock in his right hand and a knotty stick wound about with serpents. Or it may be portrayed as a maiden sitting on an eagle, the symbol of that which grows ever stronger and longer-lived (which Medicine seeks to accomplish). On her head is a wreath of laurel. In one hand she holds a rod wound about with a serpent—the knotty staff of Aesculapius. In the other she holds a wicker-basket in which she collects flowers and herbs to be made into medicines by her genius. About her are visible retorts and other glass instruments useful in chemistry.

Melancholia (Melancholy)

A figure leans on a rock and supports her head on her hand. Nearby is a funereal owl.

Memoria (Recollection)

A figure with her finger laid against her forehead while reflecting upon the contents of the book which she is holding open in her hand. Or a figure dressed in black who holds a pen in her right hand and a book in her left.

Memoria beneficiorum (The Recollection of favors). A figure with a wreath of hemp, who holds a club in her right hand and who stands between a lion and eagle.

Mendacium (Falseness)

A figure dressed in white and black, remarkable for his masked appearance and ways of speaking, holding a dark lantern in his hand. On it may be represented by an infant near a table on which is seen a chameleon which is constantly changing color. The eyes of the infant are blindfolded. In its right hand it holds a weather vane, the kind usually placed on the peak of a roof to tell the direction of wind, but which also may indicate that falseness is never stable, and always changing. The arrows of false witness are lying next to a bow. They do great injury to many. The infant carries a quiver full of these darts. The same infant treads upon the Ten Commandments, by which is meant that falseness does not respect the law.

Mercatura (Commerce)

A figure with a purse, caduceus and the wings of Mercury.

Mercurius Planeta (The Planet Mercury)

A figure wearing wings on his cap and on his feet who carries a caduceus in his hand.

Metaphysica (Metaphysics)

A female figure with a crown and eyes veiled who holds a scepter in her hand. Near her feet are a water clock and a globe.

Miseria (Distress)

A figure who carries a shield on which is painted a woman sitting on a heap of straw while dogs lick her sores.

Misericordia (Compassion)

A figure wearing a crown of olive leaves who holds out her left hand while holding in her right a branch of cedar. At her feet a jackdaw is sitting. At one side are placed loaves of bread and a plate filled money. Or she may distribute alms, holding on her arm a branch of Punic apples, fruits which are not so tasty as they look. [Apparently Lang is here implying that the fruit of charity is not as sweet as that earned by one's own hand. "Punic apples" were a variety of artificial fruit, perhaps of glass, for the Phoenician ancestors of the Carthaginians were famous as workers in glassware.] See also *Benignitas* (Kindness) and *Liberalitas* (Liberality).

Modestia (Modesty)

A figure dressed in white with little decoration on her head who enjoys no ornamentation beyond a golden belt. She tilts her head somewhat towards the ground and holds a scepter at whose end is an orb.

Momus (Censure and Ridicule)

A thin, pallid figure who stares at the ground. He supports himself by a stick.

Monarchia (Monarchy)

A hero with serious mien surrounded by the sun's rays, whose entire body is sparkling with gems. In his hand he clutches a triple scepter. On his right side a dragon crowds against a lion, while on his left many prisoners bound in chains are huddling together. Or it may be shown as Cyrus in military dress. Below and under his feet Themistocles overcomes Xerxes who is joining Asia to Europe with a bridge of ships. Or else Julius Caesar may be represented with an augur's staff and a star. Beneath him the Battle of Pharsalia may be shown.

Mundus (The World)

May be depicted by a snake biting its own tail. Or a man in a long robe bearing a golden terrestrial sphere.

Mundana Felicitas (Worldly Happiness) or worldly devotion may be indicated by a game of ball.

Mundi Contemptus (Scorn of the World) may be a man in armor who treads upon a crown while gazing at the heavens. He holds a spear in his right hand and a palm in his left. See also *Amor mundi* (Love of the World) and *Honor mundi* (Worldly Honor).

Musica (Music)

A woman whose costume is ornamented with musical notes and who is crowned with flowers. She strikes a lyre. Near her feet are set various musical instruments. Or she may be a gaily dressed woman with a horn in her right hand. In her left nightingales are revealed and a harp on which a cricket is sitting.

N

Natura (Nature)

A scene in which infants are hastening to that place from whence milk flows. Or a figure who may have a vulture on his hand. See also *Lex Naturae* (Natural Law).

Nautica Ars (Seamanship)

A winged figure sitting on an anchor carries a sea chest under his arm. Or a deity is portrayed together with a chart of the oceans and a sea chest. In his hand he carries a fish lying on its belly, by which is meant that a ship should be constructed on the lines of a fish. A ship's tiller and various trade goods are placed to one side.

Necessitas (Necessity)

A figure who bears a hammer in his right hand and a bunch of sticks in the other.

Neglegentia (Negligence)

A figure dressed in a shapeless, neglected and torn costume carelessly shakes her few remaining hairs while carrying in her hand an inverted hourglass. The sand is not flowing.

Nobilitas (Nobility)

A figure in a long dress holding a spear in one hand and a statue of Minerva in the other. Two crowns are at her feet. Or a figure with a star on her head who holds out the insignia appropriate to one in whom nobility is evident.

Nox (Night)

A figure in cerulean blue replete with stars, with a crown of poppies on her head. She is winged and carries a poppy in her hand.

Numen (Divinity)

See *Divinitas* (Divinity).

O

Obedentia (Obedience)

A person who bends her knees and raises her eyes to heaven while offering her arms for a bridle which is descending from heaven. Or a figure may carry a crucifix in her right hand and a scepter in her left on which is inscribed: *Suave* (Pleasant). Rays are also descending from the heavens.

Occasio (Opportunity)

A woman with hair on her forehead but bald on the back of her head. She raises one leg as if about to fly in the air, while the other steps on a wheel. She holds a razor in her hand.

Oeconomia (Economy)

A figure of venerable appearance with a crown of olive leaves, who holds a pair of compasses in her left hand and a long whip, such as horsemen use, in her right. A tiller of a ship may be added on one side. Or she may hold a plow with her left hand and a staff in her right while posing against the side of a wagon.

Opulentia (Opulence)

A figure surrounded by vessels full of gold and silver. Nearby is a fleecy sheep.

Oratio (Eloquence)
or Preces (Entreaty)

A figure dressed in white directs her eyes and extends her arms heavenward. She holds in her hand a box of incense. Or it may be represented by a kneeling figure with a flame emanating from her mouth who holds a heart in her left hand from which a similar flame is erupting. With her right hand she offers incense to heaven.

Otium (Ease)
or Otiositas (Sloth)

A poorly dressed boy lies on the ground. His hand which have become feeble with disuse are clasped. Or it may be represented by a woman with loose, tangled hair and rent clothing who leans her head back against a tree, and, thus sitting, places her hands in her lap. Behind her an image of Time becomes visible, who displays a mendicant's staff, a whip and shackles for the feet.

P

Pallas

An armored figure with a golden crested helmet. A rooster or a night-owl sits on the helmet. On her shield or round target (*clypseum*), or perhaps on her breastplate, she may display the head of Medusa. Or she may also have a twisted crown of olive leaves on her head.

Parsimonia (Parsimony)

A figure in a simple garment who holds a pair of compasses in her right hand and a purse displaying this motto in her left: *In melius servat* (It is better to save).

Patientia (Patience)

A gloomy woman carries a yoke on her shoulders. With hands folded she makes her way through thorns. Or else a figure dressed in pauper's garments, her hands bound, may sit on a rock and gaze at the heavens.

Paupertas (Poverty)

A poorly dressed figure who has her right hand tied to a block of stone while her left has wings.

Pax (Peace)
or Pacificus (Peace-making)

A figure treads all sorts of weapons underfoot. Also on the ground an armored figure lies prostrate and holds up a torch which the figure of Peace tries to quench with water. Or she may set fire to a pile of arms with a lighted torch near which Psalm 45 is seen: *Arcum conteret, et confrignet arma, et scuta comburet igni* ("He breaks the bow and shatters the spear and burns the chariots with fire," Psalm 45:9). Or it may be represented by a figure carrying an olive branch in one hand and a cornucopia or caduceus in the other, because war ruins all these things while peace is their protection. There are seven marks by which Peace can be identified: 1. A purse swollen with gold, 2. A heap of grain, 3. A leafy bough, 4. A bowl of wine surrounded by a wreath of vine leaves, 5. A horn-of-plenty filled with various kinds of fruits, 6. A tender kid, 7. A hive of bees. Or else, Peace may carry an olive branch in one hand and a caduceus in the other, while at her feet is a pile of weapons and a lion lying down with a lamb. Or Vulcan turning weapons into plowshares displays a hope of impending peace.

Pacis Conciliator (A Promoter of Peace) is rendered by a young man bearing a sword and a torch who steps upon a Fury. He ties hearts together while Divine Grace spreads its rays upon him from a cornucopia (from whence comes prosperity), and sets a crown upon his head.

Peccatum (Sin)

A blind youth dressed in black, encircled by a snake. Another snake is consuming his heart. For *Dolor de peccato* (The Anguish of Sinning), see *Poenitentia* (Penitence).

Peccati Servitus (In Servitude to Sin)

A one-eyed man, his head covered by a liberty cap, who is menaced by a screech owl. He carries his very heavy burden upon his shoulders while his feet are in fetters. He is standing upon a crown. A skull is placed in such a fashion that it may observe the Ten Commandments at the man's feet.

Peccatum caecitas (Blind Sinfulness). A blind man with bound feet is led by another blind man. A night-wandering screech owl perches on his fingers. Thunderbolts are frequently seen above, the sure signs of divine anger.

Perfidia (Faithlessness)

A figure dressed in black holds a serpent in each hand.

Pertinacia (Obstinacy)

A figure dressed in black whose tunic is wound about with ivy. Her face is veiled and under her arm she holds the head of an ass.

Pestis (Plague)

A horrible figure dressed in black, heavy of body on which blood-red marks appear. Her face is veiled and her arms and feet are bare. She carries a terrible scourge in her right hand.

Philautia (Love of Self)
or *Homo sibi ipsi placens* (A Man Who is Pleased with Himself Alone)

An ape, ornamented with a wreath, regards himself in a mirror. See *Amor Suiipsius* (Self-Love).

Philosophia (Philosophy)

A philosopher meditating intently and profoundly sits at a table at which, according to ancient custom, a lantern and a skull are placed. For the genuine mode of philosophic study is the same as the act of contemplating death. Nearby are located two globes with various books and a caduceus of Mercury. At the rear is a winged statue of Female Virtue with a sun painted on her breast and a laurel-wreathed helmet. She holds a lance, while above her head a laurel tree spreads its branches. Or, in her right hand she may hold a book and in her left a scepter. On her breast a large letter "T" is painted, and at the bottom of her robe a "P", perhaps standing for T(*estis*) or T(*emplum*) P(*hilosophiae*): the witness, or temple of philosophy. In between each of these letters a ladder is drawn. (Once philosophers wore robes of ankle length and had long beards and tall hats as symbols of their calling.) In one hand the figure holds a sphere and in the other a book.

Pictura (the Art of Painting)

A figure holds a brush in her right hand and in the left a rod on which is a many-hued oyster shell.

Pietas (Devotion)

A figure whose head is surrounded by flames instead of hair. Her shoulders are winged. Her left hand is pressed against her breast and her right holds a cornucopia from which various kinds of fruit are falling.

Pietas in Patriam (Patriotism) is depicted as a young hero with flames behind him and a whirlwind before. He carries in one hand a wreath of grasses, and in the other branches of oak. Under his feet are various sorts of weapons. The stork also may be depicted as a symbol of loyalty, as well as the devoted Aeneas who bore his father Anchises on this shoulders when he fled from Troy.

Pigritia (Laziness)

See *Otium* (Ease), *Otiositas* (Sloth)

Piscatio (Angling)

A figure dressed in blue with a hook from which dangles a fish that he has just caught. He carries a goose in the other hand.

Planeta (The Planets)

See *Luna* (Moon), *Mars*, *Jupiter*, *Mercurius*, *Saturnus*, etc.

Poenitentia (Penitence)

A figure crowned with hyssop. With one hand she carries a branch of olive, in the other a discipline, as they call it—a whip, and a sheet of paper containing the words: *Delictum meum congnitum tibi feci* ("I have done wrong and have made my wrong known to you," Psalm 31:5). Or else a representation of a figure whose heart is eaten with worms. In her hand is a paper: *Cor contritum et humiliatum Deus non despicies* ("God does not despise a contrite and humble heart," Psalm 51:17).

Poenitentia dilata (Delayed Penitence). A peasant stands in a field and leans on a spade waiting for rain to fall. In one hand he holds a crow, the figure of wickedness and sin (which repeatedly cries "*cras, cras,*" [Latin for "tomorrow, tomorrow"] which is picked up and repeated by other crows). [Perhaps Lang was thinking of the German proverb: "'Morgen, morgen nur nicht heute,' sagen alle faule Leute." ("'Tomorrow, tomorrow but not today,' all the lazy people say.")] In the same way penitence and reform are deferred until the morrow. At the rear is an olive tree with the Tables of Law overturned. Lightening is seen overhead.

Poeta festivus (The Playwright of Comedy)

Cujus vena vino fluente fluit (Whose veins flow with sparkling wine). A man crowned with laurel, his right hand raised to his head in thought, is seated on a dolphin. He has a lyre of Apollo in his lap, while in his left hand he holds Bacchus' glass filled with wine.

Potentia (Power)

A figure studded with diadems holds a scepter in his right hand and a golden apple in his left. Or it may be protrayed by having an arm stretch out of a cloud and offer a sword and a shield on which is written: *Omnis potestas a Deo* ("All power is from God"), or perhaps *per me Regnes regnant* ("Through Me kings reign," Proverbs 8:15).

Prodigalitas (Wastefulness)

A figure richly dressed and crowned, who pours out money from purses.

Providentia Divina (Divine Providence)

A figure carries a spear in her left hand and a scepter in her right with the world at her feet on which an eagle is perched. Or a figure armed with spear and a round shield, stands on a globe on which an eagle is depicted. Or else she carries a scepter on which is an orb.

Prudentia (Prudence)

A crowned figure holds a scepter woven about with mulberry in her left hand while moving her right hand on a globe placed upon her knees. Standing to one side is a crane which carries a stone in its claws. Or it may be rendered by a figure crowned with a wreath of mulberry who carries an arrow in her right hand. Or else it may be a figure with two faces, wearing a golden helmet and crowned with a mulberry wreath. A deer is at one side. In her left hand is a mirror and in her right an arrow. A snake is visible near her feet.

Pudicitia (Chastity)

A sitting matron with her head covered. In her right hand she holds a veil or a shawl, and in her left a scepter.

Pyrotechnia Ars (Pyrotechnical Display)

A youth who grasps a skyrocket in one hand while the other holds a thunderbolt of Jove. Near him a tutelary deity stands and blows upon a glowing coal. By this you may know that it is not possible to make fire unless air is present. At his feet are fire bombs and a small tube is also present which may discharge fireballs. [These terms refer to different forms of firecrackers.]

Q

Querimonia (Complaint)

Is rendered by a figure with hands and arms folded who has a horned owl sitting upon her head.

Quies (Repose)

A figure, sitting upon a block of stone in the shape of a cube, who carries a plumbbob.

R

Rebellio (Rebellion)

A rebellious angel standing on a yoke, who carries in her right hand a short sword and in her left a small oval targe or shield of the period of Numa Pompilius, according to legend, the second king of ancient Rome who lived *circa* 715–673 B.C.

Religio (Piety)

A figure covered with a scarf who holds in her left hand a dish filled with glowing coals and in her right hand a book and a cross. On her right hand an elephant may be rendered. Or else Piety can be represented by a figure dressed in a white garment reaching to her ankles, and a great cloak of cerulean blue studded with stars. She is crowned with flowers. On her breast a sun may be seen, and she carries a tall cross. See also *Pietas* (Devotion).

Risus (Laughter)

A boy crowned with particolored feathers and wearing particolored garments decorated with flowers. He displays in his left hand a ridiculous mask.

Roma Sancta (Rome, the Holy City)

A figure firmly carries a lance in her right hand, displays a representation of the crucifixion, and wears a garland of flowers on her head above which an oval pearl is seen. She sits on a dragon and has a shield in her left hand on which are the insignia of the Church, namely keys placed cross-wise. One is gold and the other is silver, together with a fillet of a pontiff's mitre.

Ros (Dew)

A boy crowned with a garland of herbage who holds a lunar orb in his hand, for the dew of the full moon is the most fruitful.

S

Salus (Health)

A figure supporting a snake in her right hand, or she may be standing by an altar dedicated to the serpent lying upon it. The snake is sacred to Aesculapius or Health, because year after year it sheds its skin when it becomes diseased and so renews itself. Or else it is a figure standing by an altar, which holds in her right hand a libation bowl around which a serpent is coiling and in her left a spear. Or it may be rendered by the snake which Moses held up, or else by a figure having a lance in one hand and a club in the other, who stands with one foot on a globe on which is inscribed *Salus publica* (Public Health).

Sapientia (Wisdom)

A figure holding in her right hand a glowing lamp and exhibiting a book in her left.

Sapientia humana (Human Wisdom) is depicted by a youth with four hands and the same number of ears. He wears a quiver and carries a pipe in his right hand.

Saturnus (Saturn)

A bald-headed, bearded old man whose head is partly exposed and partly covered. He is armed with a scythe in his right hand. In his left he bears a serpent forming a circle by biting its own tail.

Scientia (Knowledge)

A figure with wings on her head, and a mirror in her right hand, who displays a globe with a triangle upon it in her left hand.

Seditio (Sedition)

A figure who breaks apart an oaken crown upon her head and who carries daggers in each hand. She stands midway between a cat and a dog.

Simplicitas (Simplicity)

A figure dressed in a white unornamented costume. She holds a dove in her right and a pheasant together with a paper about its head on which is written: *Doce me facere voluntatem tuam, quia Deus meus es tu* ("Teach me to make Your will mine, for You are my God," Psalm 143:10).

Sinceritas (Sincerity)
or *Candor* (Honesty)

A figure having a costume woven of fine threads, who carries a candle inside a lantern in her left hand and a broken mask in her other. Or a figure in a snow-white dress with a wreath of lilies on her head and golden fringes on the hem of her dress, who carries a spear, a mirror, and other worldly ornaments. Or else a figure in golden garments with a heart in her left hand and a dove in her right.

Solitudo (Solitude) or
Vita Solitaria (Solitary Life)

A figure placed among trees and and mountains with flowers at her feet. For those who love the solitary life are not touched by the cares of the immediate world of pleasure. You may see an open book and a celestial globe before her. She wipes away her tears with a handkerchief. At her feet is a turtle who lives alone and keeps to himself in his own shell. Such is the wont of hermits who deliberately afflict themselves with the life of solitude.

Sors (Destiny)

A blind figure in particolor whose right hand clasps a golden crown and a purse, and whose left hand holds a noose.

Speculator (A Spy)

A man wrapping himself in a cloak which is full of golden eyes. He carries a dark lantern which can obscure its light. A dog runs before him.

Spes (Hope)

A figure in green bears a plant sprouting three leaves, for hope is fruit in a plant. Or a winged figure leans against an anchor. Or else a figure crowned with sprays of flowers leans upon an anchor. She carries lilies in her right hand and stalks of grain in her left.

Spes irritata (Vain Hope). An eel escapes from the hand of a youth who is casting hook and line into a river. To one side is a broken anchor. A crab crawls upon the floor of the dock or pier.

Status Politici Ratio (Political Theory)
or *Ratio Status* (Statesmanship)

A warrior protected by a short cloak in which many eyes and ears are evident. He carries a goad or long wand in his left hand and leans upon a lion with his right.

Superbia (Haughtiness)

A figure carrying a peacock in her hand. Under her feet is set a globe.

Sychophantia (Sycophancy) or
Calumnia (Calumny) and *Obtrectatio* (Disparagement)

Flames are streaming from a man's mouth. Under his cloak he wears a sword he secretly draws. At his feet is a money bag which a viper or snake is encircling.

T

Tellus (Earth)

Is depicted in the likeness of Mother Berecynthia, with a castellated crown who has in her possession the horns of the Amalthine goat. The lower part of her costume is the color of rust, the upper, green. Or she may hold a globe in her right hand.

Temeritas (Rashness)

Is expressed through giants who wage war on the gods above them by hurling mountainous rocks at them.

Temperantia (Moderation)

A figure dressed in white or purple who displays a palm in her right hand and a bridle in her left. Or she may be seen mixing wine with water.

Tempus (Time)

An old man in robes of various colors, with a garland of all kinds of flowers and spikes of grain about his head, carries in his right hand a winged serpent biting its tail with its mouth, and in his left the circle of the Zodiac. Or it may be depicted by Saturn with a scythe in his hand and wearing an hourglass (*Clepsammidion*) on his head.

Theologia (Theology)

A figure seated at a celestial globe who displays a crown on her head and a sun disk in her hand (for the mind is illuminated by theology). Bees are flying from her mouth, signifying the sweetest of doctrines. At one side an open book rests on a square pedestal. Or theology may be represented with a double face, one watching heaven, the other the earth, and sitting on a celestial globe. Her right hand is laid upon her breast, the left may hold a fringe. A wheel may be set nearby.

Theoria (Theory) or Meditatio (Contemplation)

A figure directs her eyes heavenward and folds her hands. She wears a cerulean blue garment and a circlet on her head, divided into spikes at intervals. Or she may be dressed in yellow and carry a triangle in her right hand while resting her feet on two globes.

Timor (Fear)

A man dressed in deerskins who has a hare in his possession. His feet are winged.

Tragoedia (Tragedy)

A figure whose legs are greaved, dressed in black, who holds a bloody sword in her right hand. Near by her royal vestments and crowns are lying on the ground.

Tranquillitas (Tranquility)

A figure holding a ship's tiller in her right hand and spikes of grain in her left to represent the sea and the land which allow their fruit to be brought forth in tranquility by fleets of shipping and by husbandry. Or it may be a maiden holding a shield who is on a ship floating upon the water. The ship's mast appears to be on fire. Nest of kingfishers floating on the billows are also seen.

Tribulatio (Distress)

A figure stands above a human heart and pounds it with a hammer. Or it may be conceived as a figure in black with unbound hair who holds three hammers in her right hand and a heart in her left.

Tristitia (Melancholy)

A figure with her breast opened, displaying her heart, in which there lies a coiled serpent.

V

Venatio periculis subinde plena
("Hunting is frequently full of dangers")

Brave Diana goes out hunting. She blows her horn and with her dogs seeks her quarry. Death all the while is at her own back. [The source for this metered verse is unknown.]

Ver (Spring)

A figure dressed in green ornamented with many flowers. Or she may have a little bird in her left hand which she is playing, and flowers in her right.

Veritas (Truth)

A figure dressed in white with the rays of the sun emanating from her clasped hands. On her head a dove may be sitting. This is divine truth. Or she may have a mirror in her right hand and in her left either a halberd or the sun. Or she may look at the sun which she holds in her right hand while an open book is in her left, together with a palm branch or frond. A terrestrial globe is represented underneath her feet.

Vesper (Evening)

Diana with one hand holding a bow and the other restraining her leashed hunting dogs. Or a black boy dressed in black flying on wings to the west. He displays a star on his hand. In his left hand is a short-eared owl. He may throw a spear with his right hand.

Vesta (Goddess of the Hearth Fire and Domestic Life)

Vesta is rendered partly by earth, partly by fire. See *Tellus* (Earth) and *Berecynthia*. Or by a figure sitting on a magistrate's chair holding a libation bowl in her right hand and inserting a clod of earth into it with her left. Or by Earth carrying a drum which contains within itself the most horrid shrieks of the winds. Or by Cybele with a towering crown sitting on a magistrate's chair flanked by lions. She holds an orb in her hand and on her knees. When she represents fire she may hold a chafing dish in each hand; to one side is a salamander. Or the Goddess may be represented in the likeness of a Vestal Virgin.

Victoria (Victory)

A winged maiden holding a laurel wreath and a palm in her hand. The former indicates the brave man who does not yield in the face of adversity. The latter is ever the reward for the vigorous man. A hawk may also be placed on her head and a cock at her feet, for each is the hieroglyph of victory. Or it may be represented by an armed maiden with a merry but toil-worn face who carries bloody spoils in her hands. Or she may hold a garland in her right hand and a standard in her left, while she is standing on top of a globe. It may otherwise be seen as a woman dressed in a lion's skin, like Hercules, with a belt around her waist, who holds a shield on her arm and bows and arrows in the other hand. On her helmet appears a cross with radiating rays. Near her is a smoking censer on an altar by a palm tree. It denotes, in the main, victory in the face of adversity and calamity.

Vigilantia (Vigilance)

In her right hand a figure holds a book and in her left a rod with a lighted lamp. Or she may have a helmet on which a crane is resting, a sword in her left hand and in her right a torch. A goose may be located nearby. Or else a figure dressed in white with a rooster in her right hand and a flaming torch and a rod in her left. A stone is tied to her foot.

Virtus (Virtue)

A figure with wings on her back, a spear in her right hand and a laurel leaf in her left, who wears a solar disk on her breast.

Virtus Heroica (Heroic Virtue). Hercules with the skin on a lion on his back, a club in his right hand and carrying three golden apples in his left.

Virtus Christiana (Christian Virtue). A figure in shining armor, a helmet on his head with the image of the Holy Ghost. See *Fortitudo Christiana* [The subtitle of a play by the English Jesuit Joseph Simeons (1593–1671), *Virtus sive Christiana fortitude*]. Or it may be represented by a young man, helmeted and greaved, who bears a spear in his left hand and a scepter in his right. He presses with his right foot upon a tortoise. Or by a girl garlanded with flowers who carries a laurel wreath in her right hand and in her left a spear and a shield on which is inscribed *Medio tutissima* ("The middle way is the safest", derived from Ovid's *Metamorphoses*, II, 137).

Virtus militaris (Military Virtue) A woman with a Gorgon's head tied before her breast, a round shield in her left hand and a spear gripped in her right. On her helmet are plumes and olives leaves surrounded by a sphynx. On either side of her griffins look up at the heavens. On the point of her spear is a cock with a serpent coiling about it. On the ground is a stork, the symbol of the militia. Or else she may carry a Roman standard with the eagle.

Visus (Vision)

A figure carries a vulture in one hand and a mirror in the other. Above arches a rainbow.

Vita Solitaria (Solitary Life)
See *Solitudo* (Solitude).

Vitium (Weakness)

A shameful small boy dressed in black who seizes a hydra.

Unanimitas (Unanimity)

A bunch of javelins tied together and two horns of Almathea fastened to it. A crow may be represented sitting on top of them.

Voluntas (Will)

A blind, winged figure crowned with royal jewels who extends his hands as if asking a question. See also *Libertas* (Liberty).

Voluptas (Sensuality)

A figure beautifully dressed in colorful, ostentatious garments. She has Love or Cupid as her guide, or else a male youth as her companion.

Urania Musa (The Muse Urania)

Dressed in a celestial blue dress embroidered with stars. [The Muse of astronomy and the title figure of a work by the Jesuit, Jakob Balde (1602–1668), *Urania Victrix*]. See *Astrologia* (Astrology).

Vulcanus (Vulcan)

A lame man dressed as a blacksmith who carries a hammer in his hand.

Z

Zelus (Zeal)

A man in priestly garments who carries a whip in his right hand and a burning lamp in the other.

Zephyrus (Zephyr, the West Wind)

A fair-faced youngster who also has a crown of spring flowers on his head. Sometimes he also has wings or carries a feathered fan.

O. A. M. D. G.
(All for the Greater Glory of God)